FIX IT

THE COMPLETE
SURVIVOR'S GUIDE TO
ANXIETY-FREE LIVING

Bev Aisbett

LIVING WITH IT
LIVING IT UP
LETTING IT GO

CORNSTALK PUBLISHING

Dedicated
to the memory of
Jeffe Jeffari
my guardian angel...

... And heartfelt thanks
and acknowledgement
for assistance
to **Dr. Don Jefferys**

Cornstalk

An imprint of HarperCollins*Publishers*, Australia

Living With IT first published in 1993
Living IT Up first published in 1994
Letting IT Go first published in 1996
This Cornstalk combined edition first published in 2002
Reprinted in 2003
by HarperCollins*Publishers* Pty Ltd
ABN 36 009 913 517
A member of the HarperCollins*Publishers* (Australia) Pty Limited Group
www.harpercollins.com.au

Living With IT copyright © Bev Aisbett 1993
Living IT Up copyright © Bev Aisbett 1994
Letting IT Go copyright © Bev Aisbett 1996

HarperCollins*Publishers*
Level 13, 201 Elizabeth Street, Sydney NSW 2000, Australia
Unit D, 63 Apollo Drive, Rosedale, Auckland 0632, New Zealand
77–85 Fulham Palace Road, London W6 8JB, United Kingdom
2 Bloor Street East, 20th floor, Toronto, Ontario M4W 1A8, Canada
10 East 53rd Street, New York NY 10022, USA

ISBN 978 0 7322 7619 5

Cover and internal illustrations by Bev Aisbett
Cover design by Louise McGeachie, HarperCollins Design Studio
Printed and bound in Australia by Griffin Press
70gsm Classic used by HarperCollins*Publishers* is a natural, recyclable product
made from wood grown in sustainable forests. The manufacturing processes
conform to the environmental regulations in the country of origin, Finland.

7 6   14 15

LIVING
WITH
IT

A SURVIVOR'S GUIDE
TO PANIC ATTACKS

Bev Aisbett

INTRODUCTION

Dr D. Jefferys, Ph.D

Witnessing recovery from panic to a point where the sufferer is no longer fearful and dependent and functions enthusiastically with fulfilment in the world is a satisfying part of being a psychologist.

'Living with 'IT' is written by a patient for patients from a patient's perspective, demystifying **'IT'**, thus making it comprehensible to all. For the psychologist/counsellor, it provides insight into the fearfulness experienced by those who have panic disorder.

Panic disorder is characterised by the panic attack, the **'IT'** whose symptoms include palpitations, nausea, dizziness, lightheadedness, a choking sensation, difficulties with breathing and perhaps most significantly, an elevated level of fearfulness and dread.

Advances in psychology and pharmacotherapy mean that a sufferer need suffer no more. With treatment, a patient is able to recover and enter the world armed with the knowledge which enables the individual to monitor, challenge and calm their own fear.

'Living with 'IT' is a ready guide of 'tools' that will assist the patient in dealing with panic and themselves in their everyday lives. It is a handbook, a workbook and a source of hope and affirmation.

'Living with IT' conveys this information in a simple, disarming and immediate form: the visual. I am pleased to have been involved (in an advisory capacity) in the development of this valuable aid. The fact of this book's existence is proof that full recovery is possible with the help of a therapist and through one's own endeavours.

FOREWORD

I first encountered my **'IT'** on a glorious blue day in Sydney, on what was meant to be a pleasant weekend visit to attend the Australian National Cartoonists' awards — the 'Stanleys'.

The sky was a flawless canopy, the yachts bobbed cheerily on the harbour, tourists snapped photos of smiling friends on the foreshore, and there I stood, struck dumb by the enormity of what I was experiencing.

Most people who suffer Panic Syndrome (and suffer is the word!) remember their first Panic Attack.

It is overwhelming, utterly terrifying and remains etched in the memory for a long time afterwards.

Hence, a pattern develops, as this book shows.

In the months that followed this initial attack, I was to return again and again to sources of reassurance, support and understanding that would eventually steer me out of the troubled, turbulent waters of this illness and back into the real world.

In doing so, and, in line with my chosen profession, I decided to create a handbook that would provide a ready guide, in a *patient's* language, to those same sources of help that saw me through this debilitating ailment.

'Living with 'IT' is not intended to be a substitute for professional help. I am in no way qualified to provide that.

I am, however, qualified, as a survivor, to pass on to fellow sufferers the kind of information and practices that were of great assistance to me, and in a form that will, hopefully, convey this information quickly, simply and with gentle disarmament, i.e. the cartoon.

My message to all Panic People is this: I *know* how you feel, and you *will* be well again. This book is testimony to that.

To those of you who may believe that your **'IT'** is far more fearsome than mine: while this is no competition (and if it were, what a useless one!), let me assure you that my **'IT'** woke me every day to the same tears and tremors and terrors that you may be feeling right now.

My thanks is beyond measure to all those who stood by me and, in particular, to one stranger who, without question or dismay, came to the aid of this bewildered soul on an unfamiliar street one dark, dark night, so long ago.

To all of you, take heart. One day this will be a far-off memory.

Trust me.
Trust yourself.

Bev Aisbett

 CONTENTS

If you have picked up this book,
then you are probably experiencing
some very strange and frightening things . . .

DOES THIS LOOK FAMILIAR?

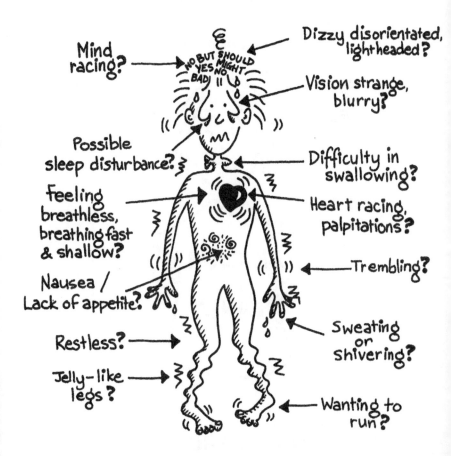

and overall, a feeling of fear and dread
that seems to come from nowhere?

Well, you have just joined
1000s of people
who have

PANIC ATTACKS!*
Also known as Panic Syndrome/Disorder,
or Anxiety Syndrome/Disorder

BUT... There is
GOOD NEWS!

GOOD NEWS SECTION

1.

At least 5% of the population has experienced
Panic Attacks and there may be many more people
who, for various reasons, keep their panic hidden.
Others may not experience actual panic, but suffer
very high levels of anxiety and unease.
With the right help, and in time, these people
can resume normal lives.

2.
YOU WILL NOT DIE

It may feel that way and, at times, you may even
have wished that you could. These are only feelings
and ideas. Both will pass. Many people believe
that they are having a heart attack instead of Panic
Attack, or that their heart cannot take the strain.
Remember, the heart is a tough muscle. It can
cope. After all, this is only **temporary**.

3.
YOU WILL NOT GO MAD

What you are experiencing is a combination
of fearful thoughts and physical sensations,
usually arising after a period of stress.

4.
AND — THE BEST NEWS OF ALL . . .

You **can** beat this!
You **will** get better!

HOW PANIC WORKS

It seems that out
of a clear blue sky . . .

. . . you are suddenly struck by
the most overwhelming sense
of terror and dread imaginable.

Your first instinct
is to run, to flee from
this agonising fear . . .

. . . You go into full
Panic mode — your
heart races, you feel
faint, you shake,
you sweat . . .

You can't imagine what
could make you feel this terrible,
so you search for a cause . . .

You decide you
must be dying. . .

. . . or going crazy!. . .

. . . or that you will faint!

Eventually, when these sensations subside and you
find that nothing awful has happened to you, you
breathe a sigh of relief.

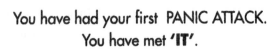

You have had your first PANIC ATTACK.
You have met **'IT'**.

The trouble is, your brain
is now on the lookout
for **'IT'**.

Since you're still alive,
didn't faint and seem to be sane,
what could **'IT'** be?

Because you don't
know what **'IT'** is,

or where **'IT'** came from, you figure **'IT'** could
sneak up on you again at *any* time,

and **'IT'** was so *horrible*
you start to really worry . . .

You spend a lot of time wondering if or when **'IT'** will strike again. You get *scared*. You get *tense*.

You become acutely aware of the slightest physical changes and exaggerate them, believing they signal the return of **'IT'**.

Your mind is on **RED ALERT.**
Your thoughts are racing.
It's like ten different radio stations
are tuned into your head.

By morning, you are
edgy and irritable . . .

. . .which makes you feel. . .

. . . guilty.

'SNAP OUT OF IT!'

you say (or someone else says).

'WHAT ON EARTH DO YOU HAVE TO BE FRIGHTENED OF?'

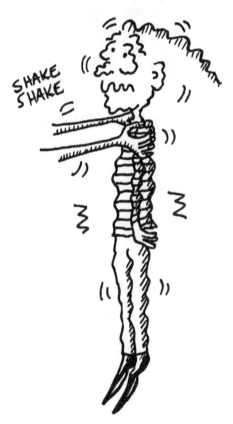

The answer??
You're frightened of
'IT'.

WHAT IS
'IT'?

Let's start with what **'IT'** isn't.

'IT' is *not* an evil alien force.

'IT' is *not* spooks and demons.

'IT' is *not* Divine Punishment

OR...

...a sudden onset of insanityyy...

_Hee Hee Hee

Heh Heh Heh

'IT' is *not* the work of a crazed ghoul who has tampered with the water supply.

BANG!

EEEK! SCREECH!

SCREAM! PAIN!

AARGH!

AND...

'IT' does *not* come from watching too much television.

However, **'IT'** can feel *very* scary (this is to help your friends/family understand what you're feeling).

'IT' feels like you're in a crashing plane.

You feel unsafe in the world.

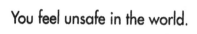

Everything that was once familiar and comforting now feels cold, alien and threatening.

Every minute is agony.
You wonder how you will
get through.
You feel so *terrified!*

You cannot attach
your fear to anything.
There seems to be no
reason for **'IT'**.

'IT' is this big, awful, hideous, scary thing that has
turned your life upside down.

BUT!!

(this is for you now)

'IT' is your *own* physical sensations.
'IT' is your *own* fearful thoughts.
'IT' is *nothing more* than this.

Believe it or not, you helped to invent your **'IT'**
all by yourself!

'IT' is *your* creation!

Recipe for an "IT"

(Serves none)

4 truckloads of guilt
16 cups of shoulds
4 bags of perfectionism
12 busloads of criticism (self or outside)
10 barrels of low self-esteem
20 tonnes of negative thoughts
80 kilos of exaggeration
1 football field worth of worrying
Large pinch of sense of failure
1 period of insomnia*

Combine with any of the following:
1 major life change
1 or more relationship problem(s)
1 or more drug experience(s)
1 prolonged period of tension
1 set of gynaecological problems/hormonal changes
1 inability to relax
1 ridiculous work load
1 unhappy childhood
1 set of sexual problems
1 family member with Panic Disorder or Anxiety Condition
1 biological predisposition
Ingredients may vary with each individual

Allow mixture to simmer for most of a lifetime.

24

SO...

you have a **base**
of negative thoughts . . .

to which you **add**
a stressful situation . . .

followed by a **topping**
of physical sensations . . .

AND...

Voila!

Your own, personal IT

Quite a concoction!

Now that you've cooked up your **'IT'**
and **'IT'** has grown legs and free ranges around
your life making you utterly miserable, you need
to set down a few house rules.

The next section will show you how to begin . . .

HOUSETRAINING
YOUR
'IT'

IT LITTER

Step 1:
ACCEPTANCE

Like him or not, your **'IT'** has moved in:
lock, stock and Panic Attack
That is the *present* reality.

It is difficult to accept this.
You don't want **'IT'**. You don't like **'IT'**.

In fact, you wouldn't wish **'IT'** on your worst enemy.

'No,' you think, 'there's been a mistake. "**IT**" is an
exotic illness.' You have a check-up, just to prove it.

But I gave you
a clean bill
of health!

Oh No-o-o!

It's hard to live with **'IT'**
let alone accept **'IT'**.
You miss your old life, old self.
You grieve for the person you
think you've lost forever.

It's not fair! **'IT'** is not fair! You want **'IT'** gone. NOW!
You want your life back! How *dare* **'IT'** do this to you!
Go AWAY!

Guess what? He's still there.

WHY?

Because **'IT'** is shaped by **you** and **your** thoughts.
So, stop wishing and grieving and rebelling and
denying. Giving in does not mean giving up.
After all, **'IT'** is *anxiety*, nothing more than that!

Yes, he is BIG and UGLY and TERRIFYING

But YOU designed him!

Acceptance does not mean that you have to *love* **'IT'**
or even *like* **'IT'**. In fact, right now, you *hate* **'IT'**.
Acceptance is somewhere in between such strong
emotions in a calm, central, neutral place.
You have **'IT'**, **'IT'** is unpleasant, but that's how **'IT'** is.
You *have* **'IT'**, in the same way as you *have* a bad
headache or you *have* a strong emotion.
It's the same as living with diabetes, for instance.
Let **'IT'** roll. **'IT'** is just something you live with . . .
FOR NOW.

Step 2:
BREATHING

'**IT**' is in full flight. He's having a field day. This is what you do:

STOP for a few seconds and observe your breathing. It is probably shallow, quick, and high up in your chest.  *Haaaa*
You may be doing an awful lot of sighing

 or panting.

PANT PANT

You are letting off too much carbon dioxide (CO_2).
You are **hyperventilating** and this makes you feel weird and agitated.

 **NOW** — without lifting your shoulders, place your hand on your abdomen and take in a big, s-l-o-w breath till your abdomen *expands*. Hold it in.

Think *only* of your breathing.
It is the *most important* thing right now.

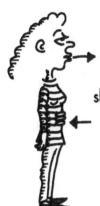

Now, let *all* the air out, very slowly, till your abdomen goes *in* again.

KEEP GOING

slowly, in ... and ... out, in ... and ... out.

'IT' is confused by this.

He thinks: 'Hang on, you're supposed to be *scared* and you're *relaxing*!!! You're *ignoring* me!!!'

Yes, you *are* ignoring **'IT'**. Breathing is the important thing right now. You are busy restoring your CO_2 level to normal. Keep going . . . in and out, in and out. This is *your* time. You can breathe anywhere, any time that **'IT'** decides to bite.

For added ammunition, find a comfortable,
quiet place to lie down.
Put on some soothing music or a relaxation tape
and continue with your breathing.
'IT' may hang around for a while, but he *hates*
this New Age stuff and he *hates* being ignored.
He'll head off and sulk.

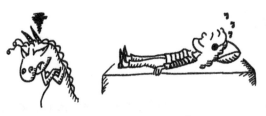

He's persistent, though, so you must be, too. More so.
Do this as often as you need to.

Step 3:
FLOATING PAST

In your mind, cast away your trembling, snarling,
biting 'IT' on an island.

You are safely drifting past in a small boat.

'IT' is raging and roaring, but you are in your boat and all you feel is distant ripples. This is not your concern because you are just an observer, passively watching. Let **'IT'** roar all **'IT'** likes. Remember, **'IT'** is just a Panic Attack, nothing more sinister than that.

Step 4:
WAITING 'IT' OUT

In the early stages of your life with **'IT'**, the pain may seem to be endless and always at an unbearable level. **'IT'** is with you day after day, and the claw of fear in your stomach is *almost* constant.

ALMOST . . . but not totally. In fact, even a formidable force like **'IT'** gets tired from pummelling you after a time.

If you were to make a graph, you would find that the panic is not really constant, nor is it always at its highest pitch.

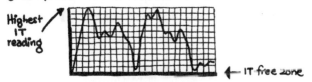

Highest IT reading

← IT free zone

There are even some **'IT'**-free periods in between!

Try charting your levels of panic on a scale of 1 to 10 and see how they actually fluctuate. **'IT'** is not *always* full-on. By deep breathing and floating, it is possible to wait for the worst moments to pass.
They always do.
Focus on that fact. Make it a chant.

Interestingly, if you were to *will* yourself to panic, you probably wouldn't. It is your *fear* of panic that makes it happen.

Return to Steps 1 to 4 as often as you need to.
They will help you to accept that **'IT'** need not overwhelm you. You *can* control **'IT'**!

WELL DONE!

Now, move on.

'WALKIES' WITH 'IT'

The first thing you are tempted to do in your co-habitation with **'IT'** is to do nothing! **'IT'** demands so much of your time, energy and attention, you feel you cannot take on *one more thing*.

'IT' makes you feel so overwhelmed, it is hard to concentrate, or make a decision or perform the simplest task. He is in your head constantly, whispering poisonous ideas. It's hard to think straight.

Eventually, you spend all your time thinking of **'IT'**.
This feeds him so he grows and grows till you cannot
function any more. **'IT'** has pinned you down.

Perhaps your home is actually **'IT'** free.
Perhaps you left him in the supermarket in Aisle 3
next to the pet food, where you first found him.
Too bad you now have to do without pet food!

Or, you may have left him on a plane, whizzing
around to all the places *you* would like to go!

Or, **'IT'** may be as close as your own front gate.

'IT' may make you afraid of crowds or people or trains
or dogs or roads or music or trees or life or death or

wars or a television show or pollution or friends or . . .

In fact, the list can be endless.
Anything you associate with **'IT'** can make
you panic again.

STOP!

Think for a minute. **'IT'** is yours, remember . . .

. . . and **you** are allowing *your* **'IT'** to hold you prisoner!

It's not the supermarket that's scary.
It's just a supermarket.
Your *thoughts* about the supermarket are what is scaring you.

No matter what you are afraid of, be it

or  $\varepsilon = $ FIRE ENGINES

FROGS

in some way **'IT'** is preventing you from enjoying *your* life!

'IT' goes hand in hand with phobias.
Phobias are **'IT'**'s tools of trade.

The most common phobias associated with Panic Attacks are:

AGORAPHOBIA
(a fear of open spaces) and
CLAUSTROPHOBIA
(a fear of closed spaces).

A phobia develops because you link being afraid with being in a certain place or situation. However, being afraid has little to do with the actual setting, but rather what you were *thinking* about and how you *felt* in that setting.

Say you had a Panic Attack in a crowded lift. You were probably thinking:
'What if it gets stuck?'
'What if I can't get out?'
'We'll run out of air and I won't be able to breathe.'

Then, as a result of these thoughts, your breathing *does* become more shallow, your heart beats faster and you feel as though you are suffocating.
Suddenly, you are desperate to get out.

There is an added ingredient here, too. The lift is crowded.

There are strangers all around you who will see you lose **control**! This adds to your anxiety. So, you panic.

From here on, you swear you will NEVER set foot in a lift again. You develop a phobia. You believe you can regain control by *avoiding* the situation in which you were afraid.

But avoidance actually means *loss* of control.

 Lifts are out for a start,

 then trains because they're confined too,

 and planes,

 and eventually, any small space.

Control comes from *rethinking* the situation.
Control means acknowledging that the lift did open,
that you did *not* suffocate, that most if not all of your
fellow passengers did *not* notice that you were afraid,
and that lifts are generally safe.
It was *your* **thoughts** that made you afraid.

Ask yourself: What's the worst thing that **'IT'** could do to me?

I could faint!

HAVE YOU?

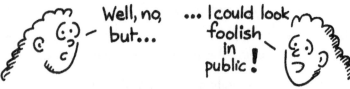

Well, no, but...

... I could look foolish in public!

HAVE YOU?

Yes I have, actually!

OH SO??

Well, people might think badly of me!

DID THEY?

Well... I don't know...one lady helped me ...

SEE?

WHAT ARE YOU
SCARED OF?

AND WHAT IS 'IT'?

SO ALL YOU ARE AFRAID OF IS . . .

How to Begin

When **'IT'** is roaring and raging, inactivity will keep
you focused only on how bad you feel.
This can create a vicious cycle.

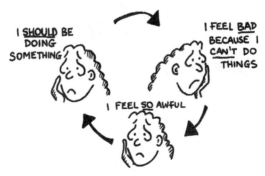

Ask yourself: What can I achieve if I act?

A. If I need to concentrate
on something, I can't concentrate on **'IT'**.

B. I could feel better about myself.

C. I could feel a sense of purpose.

D. I could feel I have regained some control.

SO . . . Make a start. Right now.
Begin to *reclaim* **your** life.

START SMALL AND BUILD UP, EACH DAY.

Try making a list:

Remember — if you are going into **'IT'** overload,
breathe. Tell yourself: 'This will pass.' Don't stop what
you're doing! Keep going! Focus on each task, not on
how you're feeling. Each task is **important**.

Doing these things means that you are working to resume **your** life. You are taking back the reins. It helps if you concentrate on what you're doing. For instance, when you ring Susie, try not to mention how you're feeling. Shift the focus.

Listen to what Susie is saying. *Ask* questions. If Susie asks you how you're feeling, tell her the truth. You're trying not to think about that at the moment. You're taking time out. You may need to talk about **'IT'** but not right now.

Oh yes, and what was the movie about?

As you complete each item on the list, tick them off. Congratulate yourself. Each completed activity is an achievement.

You did not **DIE** or even **FAINT!**

Nothing **HORRIBLE** happened to you!

You were still able to do things . . .

Despite feeling scared!!

Therefore . . .

feels scared, but
does things
= things done
despite feeling
scared
= things done
anyway!

FEELING SCARED IS NOT IMPORTANT

Believe it or not, one day you will be doing something and you'll realise you've **forgotten** to be scared!

Hang on, something's missing...

Eventually...

THE
PHYSICAL
'IT'

One of the reasons why **'IT'** keeps popping up is that your mind confuses natural **physical** changes — especially **stress** reactions — with the first signs of impending **Panic Attack**.

ABOUT STRESS

As humans, we first learned about stress when our survival depended on it.

If a dinosaur in a bad mood happened to cross your path, your mind would flash signals to alert your body to act in your own best interests.

Your body was prepared for 'flight' (fleeing) or fight — to act in response to danger.

There may be no more dinosaurs, but our response to outside stressors remains the same.

The heart rate increases, pumping blood into the muscles, the stomach tightens to move blood toward the extremities, you sweat to cool the skin and there is a rush of adrenalin, which causes shaking.

Stress reactions can also be triggered by pleasant sensations, such as anticipation, excitement, sexual arousal or exercise.

So — these feelings are neither good nor bad, but the way we **perceive** them is subject to the situations we **associate** them with.

Stress reactions occur with:

 ANXIETY

 EXERTION

and

EXCITEMENT

At the start of this book, you saw the range of symptoms associated with Panic Syndrome.

All of these reactions occur because we **perceive** danger and our bodies get prepared to take on the dinosaur, the **'IT'**. However, a Panic Attack is a false alarm. There is no external threat, so a vicious cycle begins. Even a mild physical change, or reaction to stress, can set up this cycle.

FALSE ALARM!!

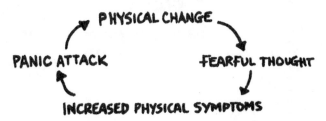

PHYSICAL CHANGE → FEARFUL THOUGHT → INCREASED PHYSICAL SYMPTOMS → PANIC ATTACK →

YOU ARE AFRAID OF BEING AFRAID AND THE FIRST SIGN OF FEAR IS —

PHYSICAL SENSATION!

A whole range of things can set off physical changes
and stress reactions.
Normally, you might not even notice them, but
(remember?) you are on **'IT'** alert at the moment,
so they can become distorted or misinterpreted
in your mind.

Some of these triggers are:

Caffeine   Fatigue   Hunger   Alcohol

Strenuous
Activity

Watching suspenseful
or violent images

Hormonal
Changes
(Menstruation,
PMS, Menopause)

Intense
emotion

AND THEN...

. . . there are the usual daily stressors of work and relationships and deadlines, and traffic jams . . .

SO . . .

you need to learn to differentiate between everyday stress and Panic Attacks. You need to recognise physical sensations for what they are — **PHYSICAL**.

There is no need to bring **'IT'** on to the scene at all. Say to yourself . . .

This is just my body's response to stress.
There is no outside danger.

Don't add fearful thoughts and the vicious cycle stops
RIGHT HERE!

THE THINKING 'IT' OWNER

CHECKLIST FOR AN 'IT' OWNER

Not everyone qualifies to own an **'IT'**. You need to be a special kind of thinker. **Try this checklist:**

I worry a lot over things that might not happen ❏
I tend to exaggerate ❏
I expect to be able to deal with *anything* ❏
I strive for perfection ❏
I feel that, when compared to others, I am lacking ❏
I expect to be liked by and to like *everyone* ❏
I am often accused of being over-emotional ❏
I am not happy with my appearance most of the time ❏
I tend to push myself too hard ❏
I do not 'suffer fools gladly' ❏
I tend not to make time to relax ❏
I find my emotions spill over easily ❏
or
I have difficulty in showing my emotions ❏
I spend a lot of time thinking about old hurts, injustices and regrets ❏
I worry about what people think of me ❏
I feel uneasy/scared if I cannot control a situation ❏
I tend to criticise others and myself ❏
I often find myself thinking 'I should' or 'I wish' or 'what if' ❏
I have trouble 'letting go' of a situation ❏
I always have to be right ❏

'IT' owners are great thinkers. They do lots of it, and lots of it is negative, otherwise they wouldn't own an **'IT'**!

Remember the recipe? Ingredients like criticism, guilt, worry, negativity . . . that's your **'IT'**.
So it's time to see this monster for what he really is . . .

A NAG

HARANGUE
BLAH
BLAH
NIGGLE
NARK
BLAME
SHAME

'IT' is that poisonous voice in your head, telling you over and over that you blew this, or messed up that, or that you're not good enough, or that you're foolish, too fat, too thin, too weak, too stupid, that you're *always* this or *never* that, that you *should* be better, but you *can't* do anything, you're hopeless, incompetent, ugly, lazy, petulant, bad, over-emotional, pathetic . . . on and on and on, nag, nag, nag, day in, day out.

He's even started to brag about himself lately, hasn't he? He says . . .

'IT' has a whole list of thought patterns to use on you and bring you down . . .

Here are the main ones . . .

1. EITHER-OR
You see one bad situation as the permanent situation. Either you're **dazzling** this time, or you never were!

2. BLAME-ME
Everything is *your* fault and *your* responsibility: the weather, the behaviour of your guests, your company's bankruptcy, your spouse's cooking. If there's a problem — you caused it!

3. ONE GOOF-TOTAL GOOF!

One mistake and that's it. You'll *never* be any good, you *always* mess up! *No one* makes as many mistakes as you!

4. BAD-TAGS

A whole dictionary of cliches and put-downs that bundles everyone into little sealed, tagged boxes.
Used widely by fascists, idiots and wimps (see??)

I'm a complete **DUD!**
I'm a **FREAK**, a **LOSER!**
Yeah... totally **NEUROTIC!**

5. SELECTIVE MEMORY

So, how was the holiday?

Oh great! I got sunburnt, eaten by mosquitos, the food was awful, the hotel was noisy & none of the locals spoke English!

Yeah!

Whoops! What colour are those glasses? Certainly not rose! Did you tell your friend about the great cruise, the friendly service, the beautiful scenery and the night you danced on the tables with 25 new friends? Somehow, you forgot that.

6. ME, ME, ME

I'll just let in some fresh air!

Oh no! Your shoes are smelly! Your company's stale!

Uh oh. The whole universe centres around you. *You* are being judged and observed for faults all the time.
You enter a room. Either *everyone* is *staring* at you or *everyone* is *ignoring* you. (P.S. They're not!)

7. CLAIRVOYANCE

Oh, the pitfalls of amateur telepathy! And you just know that facial flicker on the other person means bad news for you! How could they be thinking anything good about you?

8. THE SKY IS FALLING!

Chicken Little was probably the first to introduce total freak-out into folklore, but **'IT'** owners make it an art form. Your mind leaps from one (surmountable) problem through a whole series of spin-offs that have you arriving at total annihilation!

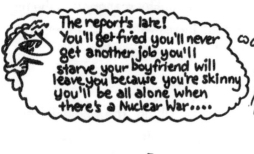

... and so on!

This is just a sample of those **'IT'** whispers that pull you down, day after day, year after year. No wonder you're feeling bad!

WHAT POISON!

What a bore! What a drag!
What a bundle of dead weight to heave around!
Where does he get this stuff from, anyway?

Notice how there are no grey
areas in **'IT'** statements.
They are inflexible absolutes:
**everything, always, everybody,
no one, never, nothing, ever,
total, complete.**

Heh
Heh
Heh

Then there are his weapon words: **can't, won't,
might, must, ought** and, nastiest of all: **should.**

And **'IT'** is so **sure**. **'IT'** just **knows**.

HOW
Does IT know?

Not exactly a reliable source, is **'IT'**, really?

Optimism
YUK!

Has it ever occurred to you that **'IT'**
never has anything **GOOD** to say???

FACING 'IT'

If someone subjected your best friend to the kind
of punishment that **'IT'** doles out to you, surely
you would intervene.

You would **defend** them.

You would seek out further
evidence before making
final **judgments**.

You would not encourage **ugly gossip** about them.

You would appreciate their **individuality** . . .

. . . and accept that, at times
they have views that do
not fit others' ideals.

You would **forgive**
them their mistakes . . .

You would **support** them . . .

You would **help** them to
find **solutions** to their problems . . .

and you would not **expect**
the **impossible** from them.

In other words . . .

YOU'RE A GOOD FRIEND!
To everyone, that is, except **yourself**.
Perhaps you need to change your **thinking.**

Your thoughts have a profound effect on the way
you feel and if these thoughts are mainly negative,
your feelings about yourself and the world will be
equally bleak. If you tell yourself the worst, then you
expect it and usually get it.
But — your thoughts can be changed, simply because
you **learned** to think that way in the first place!
It's a matter of **re-educating** yourself to think differently.
Listen in: what are you **telling** yourself?

STEPS TOWARDS CHANGING YOUR THINKING

Let's do a bit of talking back to **'IT'**! He's held the floor
for ages now, **unchallenged**. Now it's your turn.
Let's start with Panic Attacks.

STEP 1. Challenge negative thoughts

Ask yourself if the negative statement is actually true,
or whether it is an exaggeration or distortion.

STEP 2. Demand evidence

What is the idea based on? What are the facts?

STEP 3. Reason it out

Ask yourself what the most likely outcome of a situation
could be?

STEP 4. Substitute with a better option

Give yourself an alternative to the worst-case scenario.
There are always options.

STEP 5. Scrap 'shoulds'

Should is a very damaging word. It hems you in.
It punishes you. Try using **could** instead.

STEP 6. Allow yourself to feel good

If it happens that you catch yourself feeling good,
indulge yourself. Give yourself permission. Don't
self-sabotage.

GO ON — BE A FRIEND — TO YOURSELF.
(Would it hurt?)

THINKING, NOT PANICKING

You will need to do a bit of work on your thinking even when **'IT'** is off dozing somewhere. As we saw earlier in this section, there are a lot of nasty whispers in your head that have helped to create your **'IT'** in the first place.

TRY THESE TACTICS . . .

Ask: 'Do I really have enough evidence to reach a conclusion?

Leave the **predictions** to the soothsayers!

Hey! No **name-calling**, O.K?

If something doesn't go to plan . . . Will it be

LOOK for the positive option!

There **are** alternatives.

REMEMBER:
No **one** and no **thing** can **make** you feel a certain way. You govern your feelings.

HOWEVER –

IT'S

It's all just part of the

We all have good days. . .

. . . and ~~bad~~ not-so-good days.

RICH TAPESTRY OF LIFE!
(P.S. Learn to love clichés)

Feeling LOUSY?

Maybe it's not **cancer** or a **brain tumour** or something **terminal** after all! Maybe you're tired.

Does it really matter what most people **think** of you?

Avoid comparing yourself to others.

. . . but you are **not** the **centre of the universe!**

. . . some things just can't be helped.

Acknowledge your achievements!

Be realistic about getting things done. Find a **balance**. **Pace** yourself.

After all . . .
Is the **dead**line a **life** or **death** line?

And, for failing to meet the deadline...

Do you like **every**body?

Does **every**body have to like you?

HOWEVER...

it's a good idea not to jump to conclusions!

I just wanted to thank you for being patient. I haven't been very well lately.

AND LASTLY. . . (but not least!)
You are not

SUPER PERSON

Look! Up in the sky!

I don't see anything!

Have you noticed something?
'IT' is not **quite** as powerful as he was.

Even if you've only just begun,
even if you notice only the
slightest shift, you have already
made progress. You have started
to reclaim your life.

BE PATIENT with yourself.
You are learning a great deal about yourself.
It takes time to adjust. It takes time to heal.
You will need to be **COMMITTED** to progress.
'IT' hates being challenged. He thrives on doom and
gloom and hopelessness. He loves lies, mistruths and
distortions.
Stop feeding him these and **in time** he'll stop
gnawing at **you.**

HERE'S A
MIRROR

TAKE A
LOOK

You **deserve** to be happy. You're actually nice!
You try hard, you mean well.
You do the best you can, given your circumstances.
You do what is appropriate for you, at this time.

Memorise this ——→

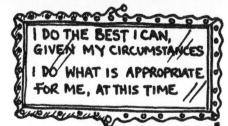

I DO THE BEST I CAN, GIVEN MY CIRCUMSTANCES

I DO WHAT IS APPROPRIATE FOR ME, AT THIS TIME

It applies to EVERYONE!

TRY THIS: Observe the differences in others and yourself without judgment for just one day.
No labels, no categories, no put-downs, no name-calling. It's very liberating to do this. Why? Because the pressure's off.

* You no longer have to *compete* with or *impress* those you *believe* are superior.
* You no longer have to *compare* yourself to others.
* You no longer have to feel frustrated or angry with others because you are *impartial*.
* You no longer need to feel that some people are out of bounds because they are *better* or *worse* than you.

You just *are*. They just *are*.
You and they have had to find unique ways to survive.
If you can do this exercise for one day, why not try it all the time? It's powerful. It's a relief.

So as a final stunning tactic . . .
Give everybody (including yourself) a holiday!

Non-'IT' Owners

This is about the people you encounter; the people you live with, be they family, friends, colleagues or strangers.

They may say . . .

Cheer up! It's not the End of the World!

It feels like it is!

OR

Good Grief! You think you've got problems! I've got this terrible...

She's not listening!

OR

You look all right to me!

You should see it from this side!

OR

You worry too much!

I know. That's what worries me!

These responses can leave you feeling worse. You feel *misunderstood* or that your pain has been *trivialised*, or you feel *guilty* for feeling bad for no (apparent) reason.

But, then again — there will be people who say . . .

All these people are reacting in ways that are **appropriate to them at the time** (remember?). They are reacting in response to several factors.

These include:

* Their own experience
* Their own personality
* Their own level of understanding
* Their own ability to empathise
* Their own ability to express their feelings
* Their own problems
* Their own ability to cope
* Their own set of beliefs

There will be some people who are able to help you more than others. Don't be afraid to ask for that help and don't worry about the rest.

However — especially with family and friends, it is important to remember that **'IT'** may be impacting on them almost as much as it is on you.

This should not add to your **guilt**, but simply be something to recognise when you can, and you may need to make some allowances for others who are going through this with you.

They, too, may be **TIRED**. . .

. . . or
FRUSTRATED

. . . or they may feel **HELPLESS**

. . . or even
ANGRY

This doesn't mean they love you less.
Often they simply do not know what to do.

Here's what they can do

(show them this)

1. Listen

Panic People need to let it out. Often.
Panic People need to talk it through. Often.

2. Encourage

Recognising that the Panic Person is trying will spur
them on. Encourage them to keep going, but never bully
them or become impatient. They are doing their best.
They need your support.

3. Be the voice of reason

If the Panic Person is feeling chaotic, step in and guide
them back to a point of focus. Encourage them to *think*
rather than let their feelings run away with them.
Reason it out together.

4. Understand that this is very real to the Panic Person. There may be very severe physical symptoms.

5. Avoid surprises

The Panic Person needs to pace him/herself. They may need to plan ahead, so they can deal with each new situation.

6. Acknowledge each achievement

However small it may seem, to the Panic Person completing a new task may have meant climbing a mountain. Remind them, too, of their progress. They may forget at times.

7. Try to be patient

This is hard, but getting angry or showing frustration will only make the Panic Person feel guilty. It takes time and effort to change, and remember, you are well; you have more reserves to call on.

8. Become informed

It is a great help if you know about the strategies that will help the person through to recovery. You can then work with them to achieve their goal and return **both** your lives to normal.

You, the Panic Person, can also help your family and friends by telling them what **you** need them to do if you're panicking.

OWNING
YOUR
'IT'

You have probably asked the following questions
many times:

Question 1.

WHY ME??

Why is this awful, bad, hideous
thing happening to me?

There are basic problems with this line of thinking.
The very question Why me? suggests that **'IT'** comes
from the outside, as if you have been selected in a giant
cosmic lottery and your **'IT'** has been allotted to you.

This concept can work against you in several ways.

By believing that **'IT'** has been imposed on you, you give **'IT'** control. You become a victim, waiting to be rescued.

In this situation, **'IT'** can take on many guises.

'IT' can be other people who make you feel uneasy.

  **'IT'** can be places that make you feel scared.

Or **'IT'** can appear in situations that make you feel uncomfortable.

Did you spot the major flaw in the above statements? **Nothing** can **make** you feel a certain way. No **one** can **make** you feel a certain way. Your feelings belong to **you**.

It's the same with **'IT'**. When you see **'IT'** as something that *happens* to you, outside of your control, you give **'IT'** absolute power over your life.

Question 2.
WHAT HAVE I DONE TO DESERVE THIS?

This suggests you are being punished.
But by whom? For what?

You are **not being punished**.
You are not **bad**. You are not **wrong**.
Your thinking has become a bit wonky, that's all.

Try to observe your thinking in everyday situations:

Let's say you've had a bad day—(everybody has them).

1. You oversleep
and are late for work . . .

Do you say:

If you made our hours more flexible, I wouldn't be late!

OR

I'm sorry I'm late, but I'll make up the time

2. You lose an important file. Do you say:

3. Your car breaks down. Do you say:

In each of these examples, you have the *choice* to either externalise the situation and apportion blame (it's the clock's, your boss's, someone's, Alex's fault), or accept the situation and try to rectify it.

The same goes for **'IT'**.
Fighting **'IT'**, blaming **'IT'**, wringing your hands about **'IT'**, worrying about **'IT'**, only gives **'IT'** power over you. As long as you see yourself as a victim, you remain powerless.

YOU'RE THE BOSS!

Question 3
BUT HOW DID I GET 'IT' IN THE FIRST PLACE?

It's natural to want to find a cause, something to pin these awful feelings on. But we are complex beings and the causes may also be complex, numerous and hidden. Ask yourself: if you knew right now that the reason you have **'IT'** is that you nearly drowned as a child (for instance), would that make **'IT'** totally disappear?

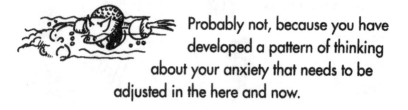

Probably not, because you have developed a pattern of thinking about your anxiety that needs to be adjusted in the here and now.

Think of all the energy and attention you are giving to **'IT'**, for instance.

When you are anxious, you see every experience, every sensation, every encounter, every situation only in terms of **'IT'**'s effect on you.

Focusing on a cause may only add to your anxiety because, again, you are making pain the centre of your attention.

Get on with getting better.
There will be time to delve into the whys and where-fores later, if you wish, and you will then be able to follow your search from a position of **strength**.

By dealing with your immediate situation, and staying in the here and now,

you are *empowering* yourself to **learn** from the past and to **explore the possibilities** of the future.

RECRUITING AN 'IT' OBEDIENCE INSTRUCTOR

Your particular **'IT'** may be a bit too much of a handful to take on all by yourself at first. He may be keeping you up at all hours, demanding your attention.

His favourite trick is to stand on your chest so that you can't breathe properly, or to make your heart race or to confuse you into thinking that you're stuck with him forever! You're probably exhausted.

SO — CALL IN THE TROOPS!

A good counsellor will help with the house training of your **'IT'**, by guiding you through the steps towards recovery and by helping you to recognise areas of stress in your life and the way you deal with them.

He/she will also assist you in finding your own solutions to problems that might be causing conflict or unhappiness in your life and he/she will work with you to help in modifying patterns of thinking or behaviour that may be holding you back.

A good counsellor will serve as a confidante and friend, so choose someone that you feel very comfortable with. A counsellor may suggest drugs in the early stages of your **'IT'** encounter. Whether you take them or not is entirely *your* decision but, if your symptoms are particularly severe or debilitating, drugs may be a way for you to get some rest, and thereby regain strength and some space to get **'IT'** into perspective.

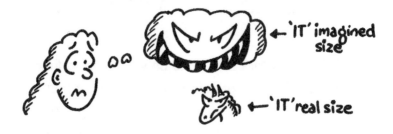

← 'IT' imagined size

← 'IT' real size

You may be concerned about becoming addicted to the drugs and, if so, ensure that you discuss the proposed medication thoroughly with your counsellor and/or GP.
Remember: it's *your* choice.
It may be worth noting, however, that the kind of thinking that leads to addictive behaviour may be the very thinking that, with a counsellor's help, you are attempting to change. By the time you are ready to come off the drugs, you will have learned a great deal.
Most importantly, you will have someone to talk to who understands how you feel, and who will be able to actively assist you in returning to your normal life.

SETBACKS

Just when you thought it was safe . . .

SURPRISE!

Oh not again! It's the return of **'IT'**!
Well, he's persistent. He's had *years* of practice.

⊙.K. THINK about it!!!

IMPORTANT POINT!

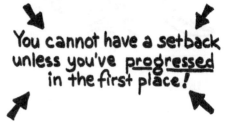

You cannot have a setback
unless you've <u>progressed</u>
in the first place!

SO—HAVING SETBACKS MEANS
YOU'RE GETTING BETTER!

You are *not* at **BASE 1** because you've already been there, done that!

You're stronger now, because you're better informed. You know what to do. Keep going!

HERE ARE SOME REMINDERS:

Thousands of people have overcome Panic. You can too.

BREATHE

Each time you feel anxious, use correct breathing . . .

You are only **AFRAID** of the **FEAR!**

GIVE
IT
(and yourself)

TIME . . . It will pass

AND . . . Hop in your boat and **FLOAT** past the pain.

TUNE INTO
YOUR
THINKING →

Are you back to old habits?

1. Challenge.
2. Demand evidence.
3. Reason it out.
4. Supply a better option.

Are you confusing **FEAR** with
PHYSICAL SENSATIONS?

**MAKE FRIENDS
WITH YOURSELF.**

Acknowledge all that
you've achieved!

Setbacks are part of the journey towards full recovery.
It is not a matter of being in full Panic mode one day,
then not the next. Recovery is gradual, a building
process. This is because you have to relearn many
things, and one is how to desensitise yourself to
situations, sensations and locations that you would
normally associate with being afraid.

This takes practice and exposure, till finally you are able to separate *places* from *Panic*, *feelings* from *Panic* and *ideas* from *Panic*.

But with every step, you remove yourself further and further from those first difficult days with **'IT'**.

SO LONG! — GOODBYE!

Hey! Come back, here!

Focus on your **progress** and not on your **pain**.
Be **committed** to **wellness**, not **illness**.

Assess what you are doing right now.
Are you working too hard? Can you pace it better?
Is something bothering you that can be changed?
Have you encountered a situation you find difficult to handle? Can you ask for help?

THINK about it, not "IT"!!

This is temporary. This will pass.
YOU WILL BE ALL RIGHT!

A FINAL WORD

It's hard to see right now, but you have been presented with an opportunity . . .

TO FEEL BETTER ABOUT YOURSELF
TO FEEL BETTER ABOUT OTHERS
TO FEEL BETTER ABOUT LIFE

You are learning how to be kinder to yourself.
You are learning how old habits held you back.
You are learning about patience.
You are learning acceptance.
You are learning tolerance.

AND . . . You are learning to focus on the things
that will help you progress, not just now, but
throughout your whole life.
That has to rub off, doesn't it?

Maybe meeting **'IT'** was not a *completely*
bad thing, after all!

If you change the way you feel about **YOURSELF**,
then you may change the way you see **'IT'**.

After all, **'IT'** is you
and you are **'IT'**.

You might never find him *totally* lovable . . .

. . . but at least you can make peace.

AFTER ALL...

I know a **SURVIVOR** when I see one!

LIVING
IT
UP

THE ADVANCED
SURVIVOR'S GUIDE TO
ANXIETY-FREE LIVING

Bev Aisbett

Dedicated to
all my teachers.
With love.

INTRODUCTION

The most important thing I learned after surviving Panic Disorder and writing *Living with **IT**!* was that I still had much to learn.

Although '**IT**' in the extreme form (the Panic Attack) had ceased to invade my life, there were still certain times when **IT**s rumblings were uncomfortably close.

I had learned enough to accept that this was something I just had to live with now and then, and got on with my life. In other words, I had progressed from Living with **IT** to living with it. But deep down, I was not satisfied with this.

Surely, I reasoned, if I had been able to turn around the worst of **IT**s massive force with the power of thought alone, then there must be a way through these **IT** leftovers!

So, I began to monitor **IT** more closely. I noted with interest that **IT** was noisiest when I faced a new challenge, or a conflict situation, or a major decision, or a potential loss. In other words, when my self-worth was on the line.

Clearly, the me I faced still had some learning to do. Sure, I was strong. I was a survivor, I was able to function, and function well, but was I 'Living **IT** up'? Not really, not totally. I was <u>coping</u>.

The me I had been before **IT** had proven to be unsteady. Her foundations were shaky, but she was all I knew. I kept reverting back to old patterns, kept using them as my point of reference. How then, could I find a new way to be me; strong, sure and <u>totally</u> OK? What were the guidelines? I'd stopped beating myself up, but life kept throwing up new challenges that I only had old rules for. What was the key?

Ironically, the answer lay <u>within</u> the problem.

Slowly, there dawned a realisation that while **IT** and I had shared the same psyche, we had never truly made peace. **IT** was the unruly tenant I would have preferred to evict. So, as long as there was a battle going on (even if only an occasional skirmish) I would still be losing.

And so, the final clue. I needed to find a new way to see **IT**, and that was to recognise that **IT** actually served a purpose! **IT** was the key to what I had to change!

It was then that I stopped committing myself to <u>coping</u> and started a commitment to <u>living</u>, entering the slow (and at times frustrating) process of education about me.

Living **IT** *up* is the result of this exploration into self, where fear became a tool for learning, growth and change. It contains ideas, philosophies, questions, exercises and principles which have all helped me to advance, not just out of the pit of anxiety, but into a whole new clarity about the world and my part in it.

I did not do it alone. All along, people entered my life to place a word here, an idea there or a soothing hand, a selfless act, a gentle reminder, a major test, some of which I appreciated at the time, some I appreciated only later. And now, part of the reward for my endeavours is the opportunity to reach out and offer whatever I can to assist each of you in finding your own way fully into yourself, and into life.

I wish you all that my **IT** has given me:

A chance to grow into a better life
than I had before; a chance to be
the best person I can be.

Bev Aisbett

How to Use This Book

1. The book is designed to help your new thinking evolve, so it is best to read it through before going back to points of interest.

2. Give the exercises your best shot. Take your time. Make them real for you.

3. Use what works for <u>you</u>. Adapt what you need to. Invent what you need to.

4. See the principles as ideals to work <u>towards</u>. Some days you'll get it all right, some days you won't. Forgive yourself for not being perfect.

5. Be patient. It takes time and practice to learn new things.

6. Keep going, keep trying, keep learning, keep growing.

7. Be <u>gentle</u> with yourself.

8. If you feel better, help someone who doesn't.

9. Do what you do with love.

10. There's knowing and KNOWING. Learn the difference by <u>experiencing</u> change. Live it and Live **IT** up!

CONTENTS

YOU AND IT

Remember Him?

How could you forget?! This is IT — <u>your</u> IT. You met him through Panic Attacks and he tipped your world upside down. You've come a long way since your first encounter – you've lived through IT and learned a great deal.

You're a Survivor!!

OK. Time for a little revision . . .

First, let's take another look at how IT came on the scene.

Dum de dum

There you were, just minding your own business . . .

. . . When suddenly, for no <u>apparent</u> reason, you began to feel SCARED.

Not just scared, but downright **TERRIFIED!**

Your palms began to sweat . . .

Your heart began to pound . . .

You wanted to run . . .

JELLY

. . . you were trembling and shaking — you felt **OUT OF CONTROL!**

You just had your first PANIC ATTACK. From that moment on, IT took centre stage.

Because IT was so scary and because IT seemed to come from nowhere, you were always on the lookout for another surprise attack.

IN OTHER WORDS...

You became AFRAID of BEING AFRAID!

AND SO... your whole focus shifted to fear and avoiding fear.

Eventually, IT became your whole world.

You gave IT your full attention, focus and **thoughts**. You know now (if you've read *Living with IT*) that your thinking greatly affects IT, and ITs power over you. Your **thinking** gives IT its shape, form and size.

Your thinking created IT in the first place.

Years of worrying
in circles, one worry
leading to another,
without ever reaching
a solution.

Years of low
self-esteem.

Years of
catastrophising . . .
letting small
problems grow into
major disasters in
your mind.

Years of pushing
yourself too hard.

Years of trying to please
everybody else (or of trying to
be all things to all people).

Years of feeling angry,
either at yourself or the
world, for all the old
hurts, regrets, injustices
and losses.

Years of seeing only
your weaknesses,
failings and
shortcomings, or those
in others.

Years of setting yourself
impossible goals of
perfection based on
unrealistic expectations.

You felt **flawed**
So you strived to be **perfect**
But **nobody's** perfect
So you **failed** to be perfect
So you **must** be flawed.

All this came from a voice in your head which reinforced your negative beliefs about yourself.

That voice was IT.

This constant stream of ITspeak went on and on, day after day, year after year . . .

. . . Until that fateful day when IT finally loomed up in all his fearsome, terrible, world-shattering glory . . .

ROAR

. . . the **PANIC ATTACK!!**

Clearly, IT is something anyone in their right mind (and we have established that IT has nothing to do with madness) would prefer to live without, so you needed to learn new skills to cope. Let's take another look at those:

In the first alert situation:

1. ACCEPT

You wish you weren't afraid, but you are. Denying IT doesn't change IT. Neither does anger, running or avoidance. IT is happening. Let IT roll. Go with IT. Accept IT.

2. BREATHE

Monitor your breathing. If it's fast, shallow and high in your chest, take deep, slow abdominal breaths. This prevents hyperventilation, when your CO_2 and oxygen balance are out of kilter. Breathing slowly also distracts you from IT.

3. FLOAT PAST

Mentally maroon IT on a desert island. You're a long way off, floating past, out of reach.

4. WAIT IT OUT

IT attacks last between only a few seconds and, at most, 20 minutes. Then they pass. They ALWAYS pass.

In the LONG TERM:

1. Keep going, even if scared

Life goes on, IT or no IT. If you avoid participating in life because of IT, IT takes over. Keep on keeping on; this builds confidence and puts your fears into perspective. You are more than your fear. You have a LIFE!

2. Monitor your thinking

Remember to keep close tabs on rigid, self-defeating or exaggerated thinking. <u>Reason</u> with yourself.

MIND READING   **CATASTROPHISING**

SELECTIVE MEMORY

PUT-DOWNS AND LABELS

ALL OR NOTHING THINKING

ASK THE O⟵ QUESTION:

What am I telling myself?

AND—

IT WORDS TO BE WARY OF:

Try 'COULD' instead.

Try 'MIGHT' or 'I'D LIKE TO' or 'MAYBE'.

Try less FINITE terms.

Try 'COULD' if you're not quite up to 'CAN' yet.

O.K. I've been doing all that. I know how **IT** works and I'm watching my **thinking!**

GOOD! You've done well! So, how's it all going?

21

Well, I'm a lot better. I know how to stop IT from completely running off the rails.

CONGRATULATIONS!

I have more control and I've begun to isolate physical sensations from fearful thoughts.

GREAT!

I'm not so hard on myself or critical of others. I've stopped comparing myself.

EXCELLENT!

ELEPHANT STAMP!

And I try to pace my life better. I've slowed down.

But...

BUT??

Sometimes I still come unstuck! I may not panic, but I get very anxious. I'm still not totally IT-FREE!

And after all my hard work I SHOULD be!

Whoops! Sorry about the 'SHOULD'!

OK. For a start, look how far you've come! For a while there, you couldn't even function! You've already overcome many self-defeating habits and attitudes. You've done the base work and you're now at intermediate level.

CONGRATULATIONS!

You've learned to think in a different way
and you're now ready to learn more.

LET'S DO IT!

THE IT QUIZ

Think honestly about the questions below. See if you can come up with your own ideas.

Q1. How do you feel about IT now?
(a) IT is a disaster that has ruined my life.
(b) IT is something I have to (somehow) live with.
(c) IT is beyond my control.
(d) I never want to go through IT again, but I'm glad I did.
(e) IT is the enemy and I am the victim.
(f) IT has motivated me to make important (and necessary) changes to the way I live.
(g) IT is me and I am IT. I need to make peace.

Q2. How do you feel about yourself?
(a) OK, I guess.
(b) I'm a loser, bad things always happen to me.
(c) I'm a good person, I try hard, why do I suffer?
(d) I am worthwhile. I am learning about myself.
(e) I have good points and bad points, like everyone else.
(f) I enjoy being me.

Q3. How do you feel about life?
(a) Life is a series of tests and challenges from which we grow and learn.
(b) Life is not <u>meant</u> to be easy.
(c) Life's a bitch and then you die.
(d) Life is what you make it.
(e) Life can be wonderful.

Q4. What do you think is your purpose in life?

(a) To suffer.
(b) To be happy.
(c) To be the best I can be.
(d) You're born, you live, you die. That's it.
(e) To serve others.
(f) To realise my full potential.

Q5. How would your life have been if you'd never had IT
(AND YOU WERE THE SAME PERSONALITY)?

(a) I wouldn't have learned about my strengths and the traps in my thinking.
(b) Peaceful, contented and happy.
(c) Ordinary. Sometimes good, sometimes bad.
(d) I would have been as unhappy as I was before, only without this extra burden.

Q6. How much do you deserve to be happy?

(a) I fully deserve to be happy.
(b) All I know is I don't deserve this pain!
(c) Thinking only of yourself is indulgent.
(d) You have to <u>earn</u> good things, you don't just <u>deserve</u> them.
(e) It's unrealistic to expect to be too happy.

These questions are designed to get you thinking about where you are at the moment. Certain attitudes will be revealed if you are truly honest in your responses. Watch for old negative thinking, or answers that put you in the role of a victim or martyr. If you see this happening, more work needs to be done.

ABOUT CHANGE...

Why do we resist change, even if the situation that we're in causes us pain?

 Better the devil you know . . . Change means moving out of your comfort zone, into the great unknown. Change means taking risks, and . . .

 . . . Most of us were not raised to take risks. We were programmed not to expect too much from life, to play it safe.

 Risk-taking involves challenging your own and others' ideas of what is appropriate. This can bring disapproval, resistance and criticism. New behaviour may be seen as unacceptable by _existing_ standards.

I hate it when he does that!

Risks also involve the possibility of making mistakes; something you are frightened of if you are critical of yourself.

 Making changes also means that you may have to finally face difficult issues and painful decisions that you have been unable or unwilling to look at or deal with to date.

Sometimes, if we're <u>really</u> honest, being ill may <u>serve</u> us. It (or IT) may give us the attention, love, support and rest that we crave. We can surrender all responsibility. We can have others make all the tough decisions, and look after us as we were looked after when we were small. We can bail out of life.

☆ We are suspicious of happiness. Two, maybe three days, or even a month of happiness and we start

looking for the catch. We watch for the booby trap or the banana skin.

If we don't <u>find</u> one, we <u>make</u> one. We self-sabotage! Anything to break all the tension of too much happiness! It can't possibly last! We don't know how to hold it!

☆ We rely on outside factors for our happiness, instead of seeking it within ourselves.
We blame others for 'letting us down' or we wait for rescue when it can really only ever come from within.

☆ We put off living. We can't wait for work to finish, for the weekend to come, to get married or to go on holiday.

Meanwhile, life is going on without us.

In order to effectively make changes for the better, you will need to set out to achieve the following goals:

 1. An absolute belief that you <u>deserve</u> to be well, happy and loved.

 2. A complete shift of focus from being a loser to being a winner.

 3. A conscious awareness of CHOICE.

 4. An ability to just BE.

 5. A total commitment to WELLNESS not illness.

Let's take a closer look at these goals:

1. SELF-LOVE

 Deep down, do you believe that you <u>deserve</u> happiness? That you are loveable? If not, why not? What is so terrible about you? Try making a list of all your good points and bad points as your best friend would see them. Be objective. Imagine yourself through your friend's eyes.

Now make out a list of your friend's good and bad points and compare them to yours. Are the lists really so different? Are the bad points so bad? Or just human?

Now . . . can you look in the mirror and without faltering, and with full conviction, tell yourself 'I admire, respect and love you'?

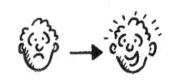

It is easier to say this to our partners, children, family and friends than it is to say it to ourselves. Why are <u>you</u> excluded from the support, nurturing and love that you need, but which is not always available from the outside? <u>You</u> could be giving it to yourself! Self-love means you're not hanging on others' approval! You're a complete unit, a whole package! If you can learn to do this, freely, easily and with full conviction, you will be ready to choose and accept only the <u>best</u> for yourself, just as you would for your other loved ones. Identify any emotions that arise with the above statement. They're your blocks. <u>That's</u> what you need to work on.

2. LOSER TO WINNER

We're back to the old 'what are you telling yourself?' idea, but this time it specifically revolves around IT and your relationships with IT. If you still experience panic

attacks, high levels of anxiety or feelings of unease, how do you see this? (It may be helpful to refer to Question 1 in the IT Quiz again to consider your attitudes.)
Do you tell yourself:

Tell yourself you're a loser and that's what you'll be. Tell yourself you're a winner and that's what you'll be. It's all a matter of reprogramming your internal messages to strong, healthy ones.

3. CHOICE
There is something precious that IT can never take away from you:

your ability to **CHOOSE**

Every thought has an alternative. CHOOSE the best one. Things happen. Circumstances change, constantly. It's how we perceive them that makes them good or bad for us.

Example: Say it's a rainy day —

A farmer thinks:

But a bride thinks:

BUT THEN AGAIN:

The farmer might think:

And the bride might think:

What is happening here? Depending on their <u>priorities</u> these people are <u>perceiving</u> rain as a good or bad thing. The rain doesn't care, either way. It's just doing its thing. It's how we CHOOSE to see things that affects us.

Even great disasters can be seen in a positive light. People often realise levels of courage, selflessness and compassion in themselves that they rarely find or display in everyday life. You have a CHOICE <u>right now</u> to do <u>everything</u> you can to support yourself, and get well, or not.

So take another look at IT.

You can see IT as:

An EVIL

OR

A Motivation

CHOOSE
every thought.
CHOOSE what you
want to believe . . .
the best or the worst.

4. BEING

What is meant by just 'being'? Do you know how to just BE? Imagine that you are marooned on an island. No TV, no phone, no books, just you. All your physical needs are catered for; in fact, it's a paradise, except that it's just you there, alone. How would you go?

What is it about being alone that is so distressing? Why are you, alone, not enough? This example is an extreme one, but it does demonstrate that being alone with ourselves is uncomfortable or even painful. We do anything to avoid this. We distract ourselves with radio, television and music, or push ourselves down with habits such as drugs, alcohol or smoking. <u>Anything</u> but just BEING. Your relationship with yourself is the most crucial of all. You need to find ways to just peacefully <u>be</u> with yourself, and to make that enough. How can we get close to others, if our most fundamental relationship (with ourselves) scares us to death or bores us silly?

Unplug the phone, turn off the TV, lock the door.
Sit down and close your eyes.
Take 10 minutes for yourself.
Just <u>10 minutes</u> for you to STOP EVERYTHING and just BE, out of a whole day. What thoughts run through your head?

33

Do you feel restless, bored, guilty? Do you feel as if you should be doing something else, or that you're wasting time? If so, this is something to think about. What emotions are coming up? What is uncomfortable about this? What is stopping you from having this rest? Why? What is important here?

5. COMMITMENT

 How much time do you spend thinking about IT, and channelling all your energies there? What if you spent the same time and energy focussing totally on the idea of yourself as IT-free, believing in that as much as you believe in having an IT! What if I was able to guarantee that you would never have a panic attack again if you believed enough that you wouldn't? How would that feel? A relief or a bit scary? If you could adopt a total commitment to your wellbeing, what would happen?

You would CHOOSE only the best for yourself. Are you truly prepared to . . .

* Be always kind and gentle and loving to yourself?
* Choose only to accept thoughts that support you and reject any that will hinder you?
* Choose to acknowledge your achievements and forgive your mistakes?
* Refuse to deny yourself any happiness, no matter what decision, change or action is required to achieve that?
* Believe, with all your heart, soul and mind in a you who is free of anxiety?

If so, you have made a <u>commitment</u> to your recovery. When there is absolute, focussed commitment to something, things start to happen.

The things that you need, such as courage, patience and determination, flow as a result of that strong, unwavering belief.

BELIEVE IN YOUR <u>WELLNESS</u>
NOT IN YOUR <u>ILLNESS</u>.

The BEST THOUGHTS
The BEST ACTIONS
The BEST WORDS
The BEST DECISIONS
The BEST IDEALS
The BEST for <u>YOU</u>
in <u>YOUR</u> BEST
INTERESTS!

IT BUSTERS

SO: How could we go about
achieving these goals of IT-freedom such as:

 Self-love   Being a winner

 Positive
choice   Just being

and commitment to wellness?

Who ya gonna call? **IT BUSTERS!**

Here are some:

1. REPROGRAMMING THE IT TAPES

We did a lot of work in *Living
with IT* on (a) recognising
(b) challenging and
(c) reasoning out the IT
messages in your head that
told you that you were a
flawed human being.

We dug out the IT tapes and exposed them for what they were:
damaging, limiting and destructive.

You've worked hard at
monitoring, challenging and
changing these thoughts to find
a better option.

Q. How can we develop this even further?

A. With a bit of **POSITIVE BRAINWASHING!**

Many of our beliefs and responses are based on HABIT. We get into a <u>pattern</u> of thinking and, because that is what we know best, we stay <u>limited</u> to old, outmoded ideas and behaviour. It's easy to slip back, unless we develop new, healthier habits to replace the worn-out ones.

What do you do when something is worn out?

 Well, you could throw it (or IT) out, but IT may serve a purpose (as we'll look at later).

In this environmentally friendly society, you could

REFRESH, RENEW & RECYCLE

 the old habits (in this case, the old mental tapes) into something that helps, not something that hinders.

Imagine a visual printout of the IT tapes. At present, that might look something like this:

If we tell ourselves this often enough, it becomes our <u>truth</u>. It is <u>ingrained</u> in our minds.

What is required is a revised message that will provide a new truth, and a new set of beliefs about you and your situation. There are two ways of changing the message:

☆ AFFIRMATIONS

This is an affirmation:

An affirmation is a message which supports you and gives you a positive image of yourself and where you're at.

By using affirmations regularly, instead of the old, destructive mental tapes, you will be changing negative habits and attitudes into new, positive ones.

Eventually, your mind will get the message that this is your new truth.

Simply put:

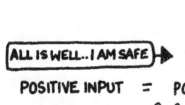

POSITIVE INPUT = POSITIVE OUTLOOK = FEELING GOOD

Remember ... You have **CHOICE**

ACHIEVING THE MOST FROM YOUR AFFIRMATIONS

☆ **Repetition**

The old, painful messages went on and on, like a cracked record, for years, didn't they ?

To get a new belief to take hold will also require sustained exposure and repetition.

Many people who say affirmations don't work have only tried them once or twice and expected miracles.

We are creatures of habit. Changing habits takes time.

For example: Say you normally drive a car with a manual gear shift. Then, you buy a new car which is automatic. How many times do you go to use the clutch before you realise there is no clutch?

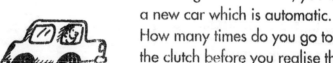

You <u>knew</u> there was no clutch, but you were still responding to HABIT. Eventually, you'll forget all about having a clutch . . . until you drive a manual again! It's the same with re-coding your thoughts. You'll need to

practise, regularly, often, and with your full attention, until the positive ideas become automatic.

How long +ill I see results?

A 10–15 minute session of affirmations, done religiously each day should have you feeling benefits within 2–3 months.

BUT ONLY IF YOU STICK TO IT!

FRAMING YOUR AFFIRMATIONS

Since IT tends to pounce on any <u>hint</u> of negativity, it is best to phrase your affirmations in positive terms.

Aha!

SO, Instead of **'I am not AFRAID'** try **'I am PEACEFUL'**.

Also, it is best to phrase your affirmations in the present: **'I AM'** instead of **'I WILL BE'**.

You are setting up a new <u>belief</u> about yourself, not a faint hope.

On that note, the more <u>confidently</u> you state the affirmation, the better the results.

A strong, committed statement will have more impact on your subconscious than a whimsical plea.

OTHER IDEAS:

1. Tape your affirmations and play them each night before going to sleep or in the morning, to start the day.

2. Write your affirmations on a card and place them where you will see them at various times throughout the day. Remember to focus on the message and take it in.

Some people may see affirmations as merely wistful cliches. We have become very cynical about statements such as 'Today is the first day of the rest of your life'. But think about what this really means to YOU. Cynicism breaks down, it doesn't build. Intention is the thing. Your intention is to feel better. Affirmations are a powerful tool, used in this way.

HERE ARE SOME AFFIRMATIONS:

All is well in my world

I am loved, loving and loveable

IT IS SAFE FOR ME TO CHANGE AND GROW

Yahoo!

I am free of the PAST & I welcome the FUTURE

I am at peace with myself, others and life.

OR You could create your own affirmations in your own words. You can use affirmations for anything — weight, addictions, money, love — **Whatever!**

YOU CAN DO IT! ←(An Affirmation!)

VISUALISATION

Visualisation is similar to affirmations in that it provides you with a new script, only this time you're making a movie and you're chief writer, director, editor, star and exclusive audience. Like affirmations, visualisation works best if used regularly over an extended period, but it is also helpful in one-off situations. The important thing is to do it with full CONVICTION. Try to picture the events as a REALITY and not just as a daydream. Make it real for you!

HOW TO VISUALISE:
1. The relaxation movie

To help you relax, close your eyes and take yourself to a safe, tranquil place. Bring into your mind all that is soothing about this location. Picture as much detail as you can — colours, light and shadow, sounds, smells. Reach out and touch things around you. Create a safe, calm haven, where you can be at peace. It might be:

Lying on a beach

Feel the warmth of the sun
(you have sunscreen on —
it's OK for 20 minutes).
Hear the waves lapping
onto the shore.
Touch the sand under your
fingers.

Walking in a garden

Smell the perfume.
See the colours.
Soak up the peace.

Sitting next to a waterfall

<u>Listen</u> to the roar.
<u>Watch</u> the way it flows.
<u>Taste</u> the clear, fresh
water.

Floating in a blue pool

<u>Feel</u> the water
supporting you.
<u>Hear</u> the far-off sounds.
<u>Abandon</u> yourself to
floating.

This is YOUR sanctuary. Nothing jarring, sinister or painful can enter here. It is surrounded by a protective shield that filters out anything that might disturb your peace.

Since you are the director of your movies you have complete freedom to let your imagination fly. <u>You</u> control:

(A) Location
(B) Length
(C) Lighting
(D) Special effects
(E) Sequels

Just as long as you are the star and your character finds peace, tranquillity and release in a perfect place. What a role!

Some of your special effects might include 3–D!
Try these props:
Perfumed oils for the garden scene (e.g. lavender, rose or jasmine).
Suntan lotion (why not?) for the beach scene. Hey, if it works!

And music can help. There are many relaxation tapes available, some with natural sounds such as birds, flowing water or the sea.

2. The 'I can do this' movie

This time you're in an action movie. Again, you are director, producer and star, and you can cast it. You can even set it in a real-life situation. And don't forget, you write the script!

Here are two examples, showing the main scenes. You fill in the rest. REMEMBER — make the film as detailed as you can. Take your time. Make it real!

Script 1 — The difficult interview

Opening scene
Approaches interviewer confidently, smiling and charming.

Climax
Answers all questions easily in an assured, relaxed and efficient manner.

Finale
Gets job!

Script 2 — The IT situation

Opening scene
A normally claustrophobic you steps into a lift. No fear, no hesitation.

Climax
Rides to 20th floor feeling relaxed and calm.

Finale
No panic attacks!

Rehearsing real-life events through visualisation can create positive outcomes in advance. You can feel yourself succeeding and experience how well you could cope in a real life situation. If you see yourself handling difficult situations with ease in your mind's eye, you are more likely to be relaxed in a real-life situation.

The more confident, articulate, relaxed and happy you are in your visualisation, the greater effect it will have on your waking experience.

Rehearsing for success sets you up for success (even if success means handling disappointment well!). We normally have no problem in rehearsing for failure. That's where all the fear and dread comes from! Well, just turn it around!

SO: Write your own happy ending! Give yourself permission to be well, strong, positive and capable. It's your movie! There are no limits in the world of imagination!

2. WORRY TIME

Allocate 1 hour a day for worrying. This is the time when you can give full flight to all the concerns and cares that you normally allow to nag at you all day. Be very firm about this. If you find yourself worrying outside of the appointed hour, remind yourself that you can't be bothered by this now; you'll deal with it later during worry time, and then you'll give it your full attention.

A funny thing tends to happen during the WORRY HOUR. You usually don't feel like WORRYING!

3. MEDITATION

Regular meditation is a very powerful tool in helping to promote a better understanding of yourself, a more peaceful attitude and a lower stress level. Its positive impact on mental and physical health has been well documented, and it is especially helpful for IT sufferers! Several health institutions have introduced meditation programs for sufferers of anxiety, terminal illness and chronic pain, for example.

All of us have meditated without calling it that. It occurs when we 'switch off'. The term 'lost in thought' describes this, although rather than being 'lost IN thought' we are actually allowing thoughts to occur, without any emotional attachment to them.

This allows IT sufferers to distance themselves from the endless internal chatter that comes with anxious thoughts and constant worrying. Our minds can truly rest and, of course, our bodies can, too.

This builds confidence as we know that we can control our fears by relaxing <u>past</u> them, and quietly arrive at solutions to our own problems, by allowing these insights to <u>occur</u> to us.

Daydreaming is a form of meditation, when we drift off, letting our thoughts float where they will. Meditation is natural, easy and available to all, at any time.

Meditation is discussed more fully in the 'FIT IT' chapter.

4. HOW, NOW?

You can't change the past. It's done. What you can change is how you view the past from the present. How do you choose to see the past?

Your past may have been miserable, true, but how many times <u>more</u> cruel have you been to yourself since then?

If we never had challenges, made mistakes or tried new things, how would we ever grow, ever learn?

Go ahead and make mistakes. Everybody does. Goof it up! Then LET IT GO.

If you hadn't had to deal with an awkward situation you would have learned NOTHING. Give yourself a break! Maybe you didn't have the knowledge or experience that you needed to get it right first time. Well now you do, by MAKING A MISTAKE! Others who have helped form your past may have been equally uninformed or unevolved! FORGIVE THEM! Does it help <u>you</u> to hold a grudge?

Imagine someone who has never suffered any losses, hurts or rejections. They would look like this. The past, like all experiences, can be seen ANY WAY you CHOOSE.

The future is unknown. You may as well imagine it in a favourable light. Who knows? Today's loss may simply clear the path for greater gain! You <u>don't know</u> that it won't!

Again, how do you CHOOSE to visualise the future? How can you be <u>sure</u> that this was the only man/woman for you? The best job you'll ever have?

Go back to visualisation for a moment. Create a movie about your future, as you would like it to proceed, from here. See yourself grieving for your loss, then dusting yourself off, looking around you and seeing a whole new option emerge. Perhaps, in the end, this transition has nothing to do with outside factors (a spouse, a job, etc). Perhaps it's something important that you're discovering about YOU that you can use to create a better future. How about the qualities of strength, forgiveness or compassion, for instance?

STAY IN THE NOW. Really think about that.

If only
If only
If only

Most anger, sadness or regret is just rehashing old hurts — even if it was only an hour ago!

Most fear is based on future projection. Hey, it may never happen!

What if?
What if?
What if?

And WHO does this impact on the most?

YOU!!

5. THE NUCLEAR WAR THEORY

What picture does this conjure up?
Death, destruction, total annihilation?
The end of all life as we know it?
It's hard to imagine anything worse,
isn't it? And yet, most of us, at some
time or other, have built up being late
for an appointment into something
almost as catastrophic in our own
minds!

If your guests are late, if the dinner
burns, if your car breaks down,
even if something BAD happens,
ask yourself the old question:

IS IT THE END OF THE WORLD??

Again, it is how you <u>choose</u> to see it. If you <u>perceive</u> something
as being a disaster, then that's how it will <u>feel</u> to you. Let's look
at the burnt dinner example:
You could:

(A) Spend the entire night
sulking or embarrassed
and have <u>everyone</u> feeling
uncomfortable. **OR...**

(B) Make a joke, order a pizza and enjoy an evening where everyone's relaxed by your humour.

Ask yourself: What's <u>important</u>? Really important? The company of your friends or Cordon Bleu cookery? It's done (even if like a dinner!). Relax. It DOESN'T MATTER.

6. LET GO

Often it's our <u>attachment</u> to outcomes, results or ideals that creates the greatest stress on us. This is the word 'SHOULD' at its most damaging. For instance:

(A)

By which standards? If you're not, you're not! Pull up your sleeves, there's clearly more work to do <u>for now</u>!

(B)

Well, you haven't, so maybe you need to just focus on feeling good about yourself by yourself, <u>for now</u>.

He SHOULD have called by now!

Why? Because <u>you</u> have decided that he should? If he hasn't, he hasn't. It doesn't mean he doesn't want to, but it <u>could</u> mean that. Guessing will only tie you in knots. Let it go.

By <u>expecting</u> things to go in a certain way, we let ourselves in for disappointment if our plans are not realised.

What if your plans were flexible? What if you let go of expectations?

Let's take a fresh look:

(A) I guess it takes as long as it takes! Thinking about when it will stop all the time just keeps it going!

(B) Well, I could see myself as lonely or alone. / There's a big difference!

(C) I'm going out. If he calls, there's the answering machine. Meanwhile, I'll have fun!

Be FLEXIBLE.
Take the pressure off yourself and others. By letting go, a whole new, even better experience may open to you.

53

7. KEEP YOUR EYES ON THE PRIZE

Most of us have wanted to achieve something and have been prepared to make sacrifices to get it.

Perhaps you wanted to lose weight. This became your priority. In order to do this, you were prepared to give up your favourite foods.

In other words, losing weight promised rewards that outweighed your current displeasure.
If you make your recovery your goal and stay attuned <u>only</u> to achieving that end, your current problems will be seen as only a means to an end. There is a Buddhist saying: if you focus on the light, the darkness falls away. This means that you don't really have to do <u>anything</u> about the bad things.
If your whole attention is on being OK, then NOT being OK doesn't exist! And there is another saying:
where attention goes, energy flows.

In other words, whatever you concentrate on, will also be what your energy is concentrated on.

What a waste of all that energy, if your focus is on your fear, pain or anger!

<u>Refocus</u> your attention onto achievement. By <u>committing</u> all your energy to that, courage will follow, enthusiasm will follow, the right help will follow, the necessary knowledge will follow, because you will be OPEN to it! These things exist for you already, just as pain and suffering exist! You just don't see them, because fear has put the blinkers on!
Reach out! Take them!

8. WATCH YOUR LANGUAGE!

Words are the fuel for your emotions. We looked at this a great deal in *Living with IT* and the progress you've made already has been based largely on addressing the issue of what you are telling yourself. However, this deserves further attention.
Look at this word:

POWER

Now try this word:

FEAR

And finally, this word:

LOVE

All three words are very strong. Did you notice how each word made you FEEL? That they <u>did</u> stimulate some emotion as you read them? Go back and read them again, focussing on how each word affects you emotionally.

Words are not just harmless toys. They are what our BELIEFS are built on. They are the fuel for our emotions.

Your IT is tuned into <u>everything</u> you think or say. You can make IT fat or thin, depending on what you feed him!
So IT himself can be:

Even if this feels unconvincing at first, do it anyway. After a while, your brain will get the message and produce a softer corresponding emotion when you're thinking about IT.

IT is not just listening to what you say to yourself, either. IT food can come from <u>criticising</u> others or being <u>cynical</u>. IT doesn't care.

All IT hears is a NEGATIVE message, and IT gobbles it down. IT will eat any old junk — sarcasm, put-downs, even jokes that mock others. IT will eat it — whether it's junk you feed yourself or junk you throw out to others!

9. TAKE RESPONSIBILITY

This is YOUR life. This is YOUR reality. If you don't like what's in the script, change it.

YOU are responsible for your thoughts, your feelings, your actions and your IT.

You can take responsibility right now, in the choices you make about the way you see yourself and your life with IT.

 Just as you are responsible for yourself, so are others responsible for themselves.

So it is not your role or responsibility to make decisions for anyone else, or to settle their issues, or even to rescue them. By all means care about others, but by helping them to know their own truth in their own way, just as you are doing. Stop living for others and start living for yourself.

LET'S TAKE ANOTHER LOOK AT THE
IT BUSTERS!

1. REPROGRAMMING THE IT TAPES

Use AFFIRMATIONS and VISUALISATION to change negative messages to positive ones.

2. WORRY TIME

Allocate 1 hour per day to worrying. No worrying outside WORRY TIME!

3. MEDITATION

Regular meditation RELAXES, REFRESHES and REVIVES.

4. HOW, NOW?

Stay firmly in the here and now. Let go of the past and be open to the future.

5. THE NUCLEAR WAR THEORY

6. LET GO

Be flexible. If you have fewer expectations, if you're open to change, <u>you'll</u> feel better, and so will everyone else!

7. KEEP YOUR EYES ON THE PRIZE

AND:
Where attention goes, energy flows.

8. WATCH YOUR LANGUAGE!

Select only words that <u>support</u> you and others.

9. TAKE RESPONSIBILITY

It's <u>your</u> life.

IT~FRONTAL VIEW

THIS IS IT

WHAT IS IT?

In *Living with IT* we saw how IT was created by your own NEGATIVE BELIEFS about yourself.

IT represented FEAR in its extreme form — the PANIC ATTACK.

But IT is not fear alone. IT, in the form of PANIC ATTACKS, is last in a long line of evolution where cousins of IT, allowed to run amok, unchecked, finally added up to a major IT — anxiety (or, for some people, depression, violence, drugs, etc).

All these IT cousins, let loose to spread their poison, built up a pressure inside. You felt angry, bad, unhappy, restless and uneasy at various times throughout your life. The pressure, as in a volcano, eventually became too great, and something had to give ...

YOU!

So, what about these cousins of IT?
Here's an IT family tree.

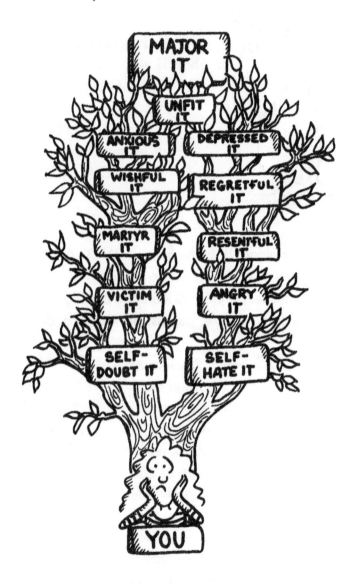

Let's meet them —

SELF-HATE IT

At the bottom of the tree, Self-hate IT is the cause of most of the trouble. He is your belief that you are unloved, unloving and unloveable.

SELF-DOUBT IT

A close relative of Self-hate IT. This IT tells you that your opinion is worthless, your ideas are hopeless and your decisions are unreliable.

ANGRY IT

Angry IT is close to the boil all the time. He tells you the world is rotten, that people can't be trusted. His moods range from grumpy to violent.

VICTIM IT

Poor old Victim IT. He tells you that you'll always lose, you're unlucky, so why try anyway? Bad things happen, and most of them happen to you. What's the use? It's all FATE.

RESENTFUL IT

Meet Resentful IT, direct descendant of Angry IT. He may not actually <u>express</u> his anger over old hurts, but this IT simmers away, reminding you over and over of the wrongs that have been done to you.

MARTYR IT

I SERVE!

Martyr IT <u>appears</u> to be very noble. He places everyone else's needs above yours, and tries to please everyone except you. What he's telling you, however, is that you don't count. Full stop.

AND THEN THERE ARE . . .

REGRETFUL IT

I GOOFED!

Sometimes the partner of Angry IT. Regretful IT spends all of his time in re-runs of your mistakes, lapses and wrongs. When working with Angry IT, Regretful IT has a whole heap of guilt to dump on you, fuelled by Angry's flare-ups.

WISHFUL IT

I WISH... ☆

Wishful IT wistfully looks at your life and deals up all the 'if onlys'. Wishful IT lives in the past or the future, dreaming of the life you <u>could</u> have had or <u>might</u> have while the life you <u>do</u> have passes you by. Goodness me, <u>you're</u> not strong enough to rescue yourself!

DEPRESSED IT

And, so we come to Depressed IT. He says, 'What's the point? Life is horrible. Why go on? You'll never be any better. This is it. Everything's black from here on.'

ANXIOUS IT

Anxious IT speaks the same language as Depressed IT, but with a different accent. He says, 'This is too hard! You can't do it! You can't possibly compete, so retreat! It's scary out there. Run! Don't put yourself on the line!'

UNFIT IT

Here's where the IT family starts to merge. Unfit IT has had enough. He tells you to bail out, escape, hide, give up. Why bother looking after yourself? You're not worth it.

So, finally we reach the daddy of all ITs . . .

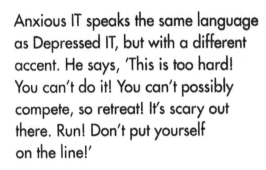

MAJOR IT!

IT ROOLS O.K.?!

Major IT is the end of the evolutionary line. He tells you you are now totally powerless, you are out of control, you've lost the plot. End of story.

Well, it may FEEL that way . . . but let's go back to the base of the tree, the roots, the foundation, the support.
Who do we have?

YOU

And the questions YOU need to ask are:

What was **IT** <u>really</u> all about?

What was the single most vital thing that **IT** was trying to tell you?

At last!
We're finally getting to it!

That:

YOUR OLD WAY OF DOING THINGS **WASN'T WORKING!!**

Hey, I never thought of IT that way!

Or the other ITs either!

We tried to tell you!

I tried extra hard!

Didn't we make you feel bad enough to change?

I guess I wasn't listening for any useful stuff!

So, it took ME to get through to you!

I guess so.

Well, would you have changed your thinking if I hadn't come along?

I guess not.

I see you a bit differently now.

I rest my case!

I still don't like you...

Who? Li'l ol' me??

BAT BAT

But you have taught me a lot about myself.

There were, and are things that I needed and need to change. Things that have held me back.

68

I used to get really angry!

Meet my cousin.

Actually, I still have trouble with that, and I feel guilty and depressed at times.

Yep! The whole IT family! And what are we telling you?

That the old way of doing something isn't working! That I have to find another way!

Uh huh

Hey, I think I get it! I need to work with you!

At last!!

Until now, I kept straining against you or resisting you or trying to push past you!

And I got nowhere because you kept pushing back!

Hey—just doing my job, kid!

But now I see how you and the other ITs work! If I feel BAD, it's your way of telling me "This isn't working – find another way"

Go to the top of the class!

All that negativity and self-doubt! Always comparing myself and being critical! No wonder!

O.K...O.K... I get enough of that stuff from Old Regretful!

All right, fine. If I feel bad, I change my tack. But how? This is all new to me!

Well, you've already done a fair bit about your thinking...

Yes, that's true. It does help.

And, so far, we've looked at a whole HEAP of other tools you can use.

Hmm... the IT BUSTERS and so on.

Yep! And I'm about to walk you through the rest!

But what about you, Major IT!? You're my worst nightmare!

After all I've done for you?

Well...

O.K. We'll look at that, too. Luckily I have a thick hide!

Right! We've got work to do! Self-Hate IT, Angry IT - All of you! Get cracking!

YUK! Not me!

Why me? Grump Grump

THE IT FAMILY ALBUM

SELF-HATE IT

Nothing is going to budge until this IT does. How are you going to apply all the things that will help you if you still feel you don't <u>deserve</u> to be happy?

Take another look at the person you see in the mirror. What if you loved that person? What would you choose for him/her? What would they need to feel better? Love? Support? Patience? Forgiveness?

Try a visualisation: close your eyes and see a you who will give you all the support and nurturing that you need. Picture her/him standing across a room, waiting to give you the help you need. All you have to do is take those short steps towards her/him and you will be welcomed and comforted and supported.

See yourself walking towards this other self and embracing them. FEEL it.

(You may have a good old cry after this. Well done!)

Take your time. Make it real.

Now CHOOSE only the best for yourself. You deserve it. FORGIVE yourself. HEAL your wounded self. Give yourself the LOVE and COMFORT that you need. BE THERE for YOU.

SELF-DOUBT IT

Think of a person you know who is happy, who makes others feel good, who is loving and comfortable in their own skin. (If you don't know anyone like that, picture a famous person, or a person from your past.) Now — are they particularly handsome, intelligent, rich?

What is it that makes you feel as though you can RELAX with them? They have TRUST. They TRUST that they are loved, they TRUST that they are worthwhile, they TRUST their own judgement, they TRUST THEMSELVES.

 A funny thing happens around people like this. You find yourself trusting them too, and somehow that spills over to you. It's INFECTIOUS.

People with Self-doubt IT problems have trouble with this issue of TRUST in themselves. It is difficult to be loved if you don't TRUST that you are loveable. It is difficult to feel worthwhile if you don't TRUST in your worth, to make decisions if you don't TRUST your judgement.

SO: How do you learn to TRUST yourself?
By simply <u>letting go</u>. Let go of having to be perfect.
Let go of having to please others, let go of expectations.
Open up to the idea that:

> I am doing the best that I can at this moment.
> I am doing what is appropriate for me.

Now you can relax! You don't have to prove anything.
Find out what <u>works</u> at the moment. If it doesn't, it doesn't.
You're learning! The trickiest Self-doubt IT situations are when you are making decisions.
Try asking yourself:

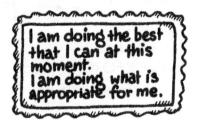

What would I be doing if I wasn't afraid to do it?

How would I like to look back on this in the future?

ANGRY IT

Angry IT keeps popping up. Just when you're going along smoothly, Angry IT can break it all down again.

We get angry → We lose our cool → We show others our dark, ugly side → Which reinforces our belief that we are unloveable → Just as we always suspected!

SO: Angry IT needs a fair bit of work.

First of all, Angry IT pops up for EVERYBODY (not just you). If there weren't Angry ITs we wouldn't have wars or violence or crime or even people honking their car horns at one another!

Why?

GET OFF THE ROAD, YA MUG!!

HONK!

Because we all have our OWN IDEAS about how things SHOULD be!!

People and situations are going to deviate from YOUR standards, no matter what, simply because we all have different agendas, truths, ideals, philosophies and politics.

VIVE LA DIFFERENCE!

This is how we'd look if we all thought the same:

BAA! BAA! BAA! BLAH!

Rebel!

SO: Angry IT is going to crop up. But the way you <u>deal</u> with it (or IT) makes all the difference.

In an argument, the problem is that both parties believe that they are RIGHT. Clearly, you want your side of an issue to be <u>heard</u>, but so does the other person.

How do you approach this?

Imagine the issue between you is a brick wall.

You could try to RAM your way through, using ANGER.

BUT

A. It doesn't work and ...

B. It hurts

OR:

You could figure out a completely different way to <u>approach</u> the wall.

OR:

CO-OPERATE to create a way through the wall.

THEN AGAIN:

You <u>could</u> keep bashing away. The wall will cave in eventually, but so will you!

How did the wall get there? The wall comes up when someone or something falls short of our <u>expectations</u> or <u>standards</u>.

IN OTHER WORDS:

Things have not gone the way you would have had them go.

EXAMPLES:

Fred is late. You expected him to be on time

Your submission is turned down. You expected it to be accepted.

The dog is barking. You decide it shouldn't be.

Of course, the same goes for the other person.

Fred has missed the bus. That's made him angry. When you nag at him for being late again, he expects you not to.

Your boss got angry when you got angry. She expected you to control your emotions.

Your dog is just confused. All it knows is that it's a dog and barking's part of the job. Your dog will forgive you, though. Dogs do that.

77

SO: What to do? How do you deal with Angry IT? What are the new ways to handle conflict?

FIRST... GROUND RULES!

> 1. No interrupting
> 2. No name-calling
> 3. Genuinely desire to find a solution

OK. Here goes . . .

1. An 'I' for an 'I'

As we saw in 'IT Busters', you need to own <u>your</u> issues and no-one else's. Nowhere could this be more true than in a conflict situation.

So often we point the finger: 'You did this' 'He did that' 'She said so and so'. What someone else does, <u>even if it affects you</u> is not <u>your</u> issue! How you <u>feel</u> about it is.

By using only 'I' statements, or 'I feel', you are expressing <u>your</u> feelings and perceptions of a situation.

TRY: I feel angry because I wanted you to...   NOT: You make me angry when you let me down!

Did you spot the differences here? The first person is stating her case from her own perspective. Even the statement 'I <u>wanted</u> you to . . . ' says that she is angry because what <u>she wanted</u> to happen, didn't. In other words, <u>her expectations</u> were not met.

The second person is taking no responsibility. No one can <u>make</u> you angry. <u>You</u> govern your emotions. No one can 'let you down', either. Your <u>expectations</u> of them can make you <u>feel</u> let down, if they are not met.

Statements of blame will not get you an open response or a sympathetic hearing of your side:

All you will get is **RESISTANCE & DEFENSIVENESS**
SO: The responses could be:

2. Express yourself

OK, you're angry. Express it! Something's been brought to a head. It needs to be dealt with. Tell it as you see it.

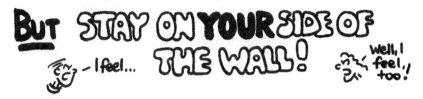

Express <u>your</u> feelings, <u>your</u> views, <u>your</u> hurts and how <u>you</u> see the situation, but use only the word 'I'.

EXPLAIN, DON'T BLAME!

You could also try a test run. Talk to a photo of the person or visualise them sitting opposite you. This way you can clarify your thoughts and let some of the worst anger out before you deal directly with the person. You could write down the main points of what you want to say, as well. It is important to state your case clearly, from a position of strength in yourself.

Then LET IT GO! It's important that, in expressing your side, you <u>release</u> rather than <u>rehash</u>. State your case, firmly, but don't keep going over and over the same issues. Then, <u>listen</u> to the other person's side.

If someone's angry with you:

Encourage them to express how they feel.
Tell them that you're listening.

It works for <u>both</u> of you! **WHY?**

a. Because there is no <u>resistance</u>, the anger is quickly spent.

b. The other person feels that they are being <u>heard</u> and can thus express their feelings openly.

c. You are <u>supporting</u> them and co-operating with them to find a solution.

So you BOTH feel better! You have something to work with.
You have the information you need, without it boiling up into
an argument. Now it's your turn to speak.

3. See the other side

Step back and listen.
What are the person's issues?
Are they <u>really</u> about you, or
are they coming from fear, or
old pain or some private
problem?
You <u>could</u> try to find out.

If someone has their own
issues, <u>you</u> can decide
whether to buy into them or not. Sometimes, however, these
issues can impact heavily (and negatively) on you.

FOR INSTANCE:

Some people are so caught up in their own poison, it spills over into everything they do and say. By seeing this as <u>their</u> problem, you can choose not to play the game. You can <u>change</u> the part that you play. You can be firm and refuse to listen to criticism. You can refuse to buy into this.

ANGRY IT BUSTERS

Let's go back to our first 3 situations and try the IT Busters:

LETTING GO

Well, I'm disappointed about the submission, but I won't let it get at me. I've got that other idea...

As for the dog, well you could **CHOOSE** to let it get at you or not. You <u>could</u> IGNORE it.

THE NUCLEAR WAR THEORY

Well, Fred is usually late. I won't let it ruin my day. I'll leave him a note & he can meet me there.

IS IT REALLY SUCH A BIG DEAL?

Which brings us to **ANNOYANCES**

A funny thing happens when you get annoyed by something.

It just ANNOYS YOU EVEN MORE!

Why? Because all your attention is focussed onto the annoying thing, so eventually that's ALL you'll see! So there <u>seems</u> to be more of it!

AND CRITICISM works in the same way.

Being criticised means that we're getting <u>noticed</u>, even if in a negative way. Being praised does the same thing, except it makes us feel good about what we're doing! So, <u>praise</u> the good stuff and you'll get more of it.

Not only will the person being praised be more likely to repeat that which is praised, but the thing that annoys you will most likely drop away, because (a) it's not being noticed and (b) your focus is elsewhere.

Who does Angry IT impact on the most?

YOU!!

Let's go back to the driver who tooted at you. What if, to top it all off, he almost ran you over?

This made you feel very ANGRY!

In fact, you're FURIOUS!

What effect does this have on the driver? **NONE!!**

He's gone! The only one nearly having a coronary is YOU!

SO: With Angry IT — acknowledge him, feel him, know him. Then — LET HIM GO!

VICTIM IT

Victim IT people give away all their power. They see <u>circumstances</u> as ruling their lives and others as ruling their lives. Victims see themselves as puppets of fate. Well, here's good news for victims. You have now just entered an extraordinary planetary conjunction and, for the rest of your life you will be lucky, prosperous and happy! All you need to do to ensure this is to repeat the affirmation below 10 times a day, every day.

RESENTFUL IT

The Number 1 IT Buster for Resentful IT is LETTING GO.

Forgiveness is the end process of letting go. Forgiveness is deciding that whatever happened is <u>no</u> <u>longer</u> important. Letting go is when you decide that it is less painful to release and forgive than to hold on to the pain of an old grudge for the sake of being right (and remember, everyone has their own view of what's right).

Ask yourself:

DO YOU WANT TO BE **RIGHT**
OR DO YOU WANT TO BE **HAPPY?**

MARTYR IT

There's a fine line between helping others and giving your life away. It's time to think about RESPONSIBILITY in another way. Being responsible means doing the best by others, by all means, but also doing the best for yourself. The two are not mutually exclusive.

The more you have a sense of your own worth, the more you will be able to <u>receive</u> as well as give. Allow others the right to give <u>you</u> love, too. Denying yourself these gifts denies others the opportunity to <u>share</u> your happiness with you.
For example, if you're complimented, don't reject it! That diminishes the other person's gift to you!

REGRETFUL IT

Guilt, like worry, is an emotion that keeps you going around in circles. It is a brain-drain, and a prison, with no way out. It's a waste of time and energy. The only way to break the circle is to ACT. Being sorry heals nothing.

<u>Doing</u> something to repair a situation does.
If you've had a fight with a friend and you want to change it, try to make amends.

They might not want to, however, and you must respect that. But <u>you</u> acted to change things. Now you can let it rest.

Even changing your<u>self,</u> if there is no access to a past situation, is acting to lay shame to rest. Concentrate on getting on with your life, older, wiser, and clearer for the experience.

WISHFUL IT

You have dreams you'll never realise, paths you'll never tread . . .Why? Because you don't believe they're for <u>you</u>. For other people — but not for you. Remember commitment? How all else follows? Do it. What's <u>really</u> stopping you? <u>Who's</u> really stopping you? The 'How, Now?' IT Buster is for you. Simply begin. NOW. Sometimes the problem is that Wishfuls are thinking too big and get overwhelmed. OK. Start small, work out a plan.

Take it in bite-sized chunks. Identify your skills, abilities, and strengths. If you lack in certain areas, where could you find support? Family? A professional? Extra money? All it needs is for you to say one word: **YES**.

DEPRESSED IT AND ANXIOUS IT

These two ITs often go together. You're anxious, you're anxious about being anxious, and you're caught up in an endless cycle. Feeling caught, you become depressed. Depressed IT can work alone, but he comes from the same stuff. Well, you're well equipped now with a whole bag of strategies to work with these two ITs. These ITs are definitely attention-seekers. If you let them, they can become your whole reality.

Shift your focus. CHOOSE another reality, and make these ITs the understudies, rather than the stars of the show. <u>You're</u> the star!

UNFIT IT

Unfit ITs job is to <u>bury</u> our pain. We smoke, we drink, we eat junk food, in an attempt to <u>smother</u> Anxious IT or Angry IT or Depressed IT.

Watch what happens when you try to quit smoking, go on the wagon or start dieting!

You get cranky, weepy or even a bit panicky! Unfit IT keeps a lid on the undesirable feelings.

The thing is, those feelings don't go away. In fact they are reinforced by Unfit IT telling you that you don't <u>deserve</u> to feel healthy.

So you need to smoke or drink or eat more, and so the IT voice gets louder, and so on and on the cycle goes till your health suffers, and you are less able to cope.

To get Unfit IT into shape involves the same principles as dealing with Self-hate IT. When self-hate transforms into self-love, it means doing the <u>right thing by yourself</u> in <u>all</u> areas of your life.

There are some things you can begin to do right now which will help deal with Unfit IT in terms of the <u>whole</u> you, MIND, BODY and SPIRIT.

We'll look at those in the 'FIT IT' chapter.

MAJOR IT !

Call him what you will — panic attacks, panic disorder, anxiety, nervous breakdown, chronic depression, violent behaviour, phobia — he is why you're here, feeling this. Let's talk with him again:

O.K. I have a clearer picture now. The ITs tell me that something's not working and that I have to change my approach. But you keep hanging around! Why?

Well, obviously you still need me!

NEED you! That's a bit rich! How could I possibly need you? You're horrible, vicious, cruel & painful!

Only because you still believe that I am. You still believe in me, right?

87

But it wasn't my belief in you that made you appear! You just sprang up!

 Wasn't it? You'd been listening to my cousins for years! You believed in them! They just introduced you to me!

 Well... O.K. But need you? That's going a bit far!

 Then why not just let me go?

 Now you're making me ANGRY!! I'm trying to get rid of you!

 Oh dear! How quickly we forget! No 1. You're making you angry No. 2. I said: "let go of" not "get rid of"!

 Just look at how much time & energy you invest in keeping me alive! Look at how often you think about how BAD I am!

I'm POWERFUL, right? Damn right! Well, imagine ALL THAT POWER used to transform me into something GOOD!

How?!

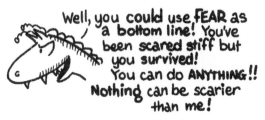
Well, you could use FEAR as a bottom line! You've been scared stiff but you survived! You can do ANYTHING!! Nothing can be scarier than me!

And you could see me differently. Look at the things I've taught you! PATIENCE, STRENGTH, COMPASSION, BETTER THINKING to name but a few!

I've given you the chance to find a whole new better you! Not bad, eh?

But sometimes I just feel uneasy for no apparent reason!

Well you don't belong to an exclusive club! Non-panickers have off-days, too! It's not a BIG DEAL if you DEAL with it!

Listen, kid, like it or not, you and I are travelling together for the moment. You can do it kicking & bucking all the way or keep plugging away till eventually...

... you get the idea that I'm not here to harm you. but to teach you...

... and suddenly...

...I'm TRANSFORMED!

Life SITuations

THE PROFESSIONAL IT

IT presents a number of challenges in the workplace. This is where a lot of your good intentions can go out of the window as the pressure of deadlines, demanding people and limited time get on top of you.

Most of what we've looked at already can help you in your (all new) approach to work, and life in general. However, here are a few more ideas specifically relating to work.

1. LOVE WHAT YOU DO

The old saying goes, 'Time flies when you're having fun'. Want to drag your day out forever? Then RESENT and RESIST your work.

If your working day consists of waiting for tea break then lunch break then hometime, and if your whole working week is just one long blight between weekends, then it figures that work, for you, will be agony.

But again, it's not the work that's the problem. It's how you <u>feel</u> about it. What if you saw work in a new light? What if you saw it with respect for the rewards it gives you? Not just <u>financial</u> rewards, (though they are important too) but for the satisfaction of doing something really well? You may even find satisfaction in working out a whole, new, inventive way of doing something menial.

91

Say you put the same doodahs on the same whatsits in the same doohickies each day. This <u>could</u> be very boring.

OR

* You could set yourself personal goals — 2000 doodahs on the whatsits before 3 p.m.
* You could set up a musical rhythm in your head and work to that.

* You could inject humour into your work — wear a silly hat one day and make your workmate laugh.

OR

You could simply decide that you actually care quite a lot about working with your doodahs, whatsits and doohickies, and that you take pride in your honest labour.

IT'S UP TO YOU!

If you love what you do, work will MEAN something in your life. If you don't, then you will be miserable. But then, you could always RESIGN. Shock! Horror! Unthinkable! How will you live?

HOW ARE YOU LIVING NOW?

What value are you to your family, friends and workmates if you feel bored, resentful and frustrated by the work you do?

NO?

OK. Fine. It's your life, and your choice. But don't be surprised if you find yourself getting a cold here, a headache there, an infection now and then, or even a broken leg.

WHY? Because you're dragging around so much HATE for your job, your body says, 'WOW! That's a bad place, I'll get sick for a while so you don't have to go there'.

DON'T BELIEVE IT?

Fine. Leave your job and find something rewarding, then see what happens. Better still, work for yourself.

Or stay put (and get medical insurance).

2. BE A BIT DISPENSABLE

Your boss loves you. You work late, work weekends, you take on everything and you know how the whole company works. So the work piles up and up because you're so good at it! Eventually, you're doing everyone else's work, too. Why do you do this?

Because it makes you feel needed.

And being indispensable gives you a certain <u>control</u>. In fact, you <u>make sure</u> that no one else knows where anything goes, or how things work, because <u>you</u> do it. Guess what? You get stressed, and one day develop a serious migraine. You <u>can't</u> go to work. What is most disappointing is that everyone COPED without you! They can, and they do! Give yourself a break! What are you <u>killing</u> yourself for? Be a bit dispensable and watch what happens. See? The world does not end. (Sorry!)

3. TIME OUT

And while you're at it, you may as well take a break.

STOP EVERYTHING!

<u>Five</u> minutes of just doing nothing can double your productivity. How creative, productive or capable are you being by thrashing on through? You end up working <u>against</u> yourself. Try meditation here. Tune out. Then back to work, refreshed, and twice as efficient!

4. DETACH FROM OUTCOMES

This is about removing expectations once again. Forget the deadline! You'll either meet it, or you won't! You'll either get there (or not) sweating over it, and working <u>against</u> yourself, and feeling stressed, or you'll get there (or not) another way. That other way is about staying firmly in the present. Get into what you're doing right <u>now</u>. Feel the difference? You're calm and productive. And the deadline? Ha! No problem! You'll ROMP it in!

FIGHTING YOURSELF TO MEET THE DEADLINE

FOCUSSED & PRODUCTIVE IN THE NOW

THE SOCIAL IT

The Social IT is about you interacting with others.

This is always tricky, because as we saw with anger, people have this tendency to do things in a different way from the way we <u>expect</u> them to.

Clearly, the important thing here is to take another look at your expectations.

Ask yourself: How <u>flexible</u> am I?

How <u>free</u> are my responses?

The more room you give yourself and others to move in, the more relaxed you and others will feel.

TRICKY TYPES

Of course, even with our best intentions, sometimes we encounter situations that really test these out. A good example of this is in our dealings with difficult people (as we saw in 'Angry IT').

Here are some questions to ask yourself:

1. How is this person's behaviour impacting on me?
2. What have I been doing in response?
3. What could I do to change things?
4. What are the possible outcomes/consequences?
5. What are the likely outcomes/consequences?
6. How would my life be without this person?

7. Why am I in this situation?
8. Why do I stay in this situation?
9. Am I seeing this person clearly?
10. Am I prepared to take a risk?

Let's look at these

1. IMPACT

How much impact is this person's behaviour <u>really</u> having on your life? Is it possible to modify <u>your</u> attitudes towards <u>them</u>? Rate the situation 1 to 10, with an unbearable situation (e.g. violence) at 10. If things are at the upper end of the scale, wouldn't you be better off out of there?

2. YOUR RESPONSE How have you been buying into this situation? Do you play doormat? Are you the dominant one? Where is your area of control or lack of control? Are these <u>your</u> issues or someone else's?

Why do you always walk all over me?

3. YOUR CHANGES What could <u>you</u> change? Forget trying to change anyone else — that's not your role. Could you stand up to them and state your position? Make your <u>own</u> plans without relying on others? Refuse to enter another's game? Leave? See another more compassionately? Let go of a grudge?

4. POSSIBLE OUTCOMES What, in the best or worst case scenario, could the outcome of change be? What if you did nothing?

5. LIKELY OUTCOMES What is most likely to happen if you make changes? Is this <u>your</u> problem?

6. LIFE WITHOUT THEM What if this person wasn't around anymore? Would that really be the worst thing or the best thing?

whew!

7. WHY ARE YOU HERE? Does this situation <u>benefit</u> you in some way? (You have to be <u>really</u> honest here). Does this person make you feel superior? Righteously indignant? Does this give you <u>attention</u>, even if negative?

Hurrumph!

8. WHY STAY? If the situation is unbearable, why do you <u>really</u> stay? Because of fear? What does that say about <u>you</u> and your self-worth?

What if there's no-one else?

9. WHAT DO YOU SEE? Look a little deeper. Where is this person coming from? Are they hurting? Sad? Lonely? What do they <u>need</u>? Would they benefit from support? Forgiveness? Understanding?

10. RISKS How much are you prepared to risk to improve the situation for yourself? How much are you prepared to do to feel better?

Use these questions to evaluate where YOU stand in this situation and the changes YOU could make to improve it, without relying on others to change (because they might not).

SOME THINGS TO THINK ABOUT AND TRY WHEN DEALING WITH OTHERS

OVEREMOTIONAL **ENTHUSIASTIC**

Sometimes the 'worst' in us is the same as the 'best' in us!

One way to 'love the unloveable' is to see other people as being related to you, like family. You may not **LIKE** what they do, but you **LOVE** them anyway! (And forgive them!)

Respect other people's right to be DIFFERENT to you

"And you should"...

SMILE!
Try it! It does work!

Giving **ADVICE** is tricky.
Do you really know what's best for anyone else? If you're asked, fine, but give the person a choice e.g. "What if you tried..."

How **interested** are you in other people? How much do you **INVITE** their ideas, opinions & feelings?

How good a **LISTENER** are you??

I don't know... tell me!

DON'T KNOW something is **O.K.!**

If we do something WRONG, we usually know it. We don't need ATTACK! We need HELP, SUPPORT or FORGIVENESS.

CO-OPERATION beats **COMPETITION!**

YOU DON'T NEED ANYONE'S

I expect you to do the RIGHT THING!

I am! MY THING!

PERMISSION OR **APPROVAL** to live _your_ life as _you_ see fit!

Develop your **OWN HAPPINESS, PEACE & FREEDOM**

Then... **Share it AROUND!**

IT IN LOVE
WHAT IS LOVE?

Ask 50 different people this question and you'll get 50 different answers.

It's umm... feeling sort of warm & glowy and you get butterflies!

Love? Love is adolescent fancy. Respect & loyalty, they're what's important!

Love is trust & feeling safe.

It's hard to define and it means different things to different people.

So perhaps, when we're talking about romantic love, we should look at what love ISN'T, or shouldn't be.

Surely love isn't about feeling BAD!!

And yet that's just how many people, supposedly in love, feel!

THEY WORRY...
Oh God, where are we going?

THEY COMPLAIN...
Nag, nag nag! That's all you do!

THEY ARGUE...
You're always saying that!
I am not!

THEY PUT DOWN THE ONES THEY "LOVE"

THEY FEEL JEALOUS...

.. OR ENVIOUS

THEY RESENT BEING WITH SOMEONE...

...YET ARE TERRIFIED OF LOSING THEM!

AND: What's the first thing most people tend to want to do when someone special comes along?

If this is love, then it's a MINEFIELD!
Talk about IT country! You've got Angry IT and Anxious IT and Victim IT and all the other ITs rolled into one situation!

BUT WAIT! WHAT DO THE ITS TELL YOU?

The Old Way Isn't WORKING!!

Time for a RETHINK, eh? Let's start!

Q. What do those closest to you do most of?

A. THEY PRESS YOUR IT BUTTONS!

No-one can show you your blocks, fears and inflexibilities like an intimate partner. Where else do you risk so much, reveal so much, trust so much and open out so much?

SO: What if we looked at love in another way?

WHAT IF LOVE WAS LESS OF:

I wonder what I can get out of this?

AND MORE OF:

I wonder what I can learn about myself in this?

Look back over your past romances. Do you see a pattern?
Do the same old issues keep coming up? Do the same old
problems keep repeating? What is YOUR role in this?
You now have the opportunity to break that pattern

By **LEARNING** from your Love ITs!

Here are some:

1. NEEDY IT

Need me! Feed me!

So often we look to another to
<u>complete</u> us. We need that person
for our happiness.

Not only does this set up a fear in you
of losing your partner, but it places a
terrible responsibility on your partner to provide for all of <u>your</u>

needs. How can that person possibly
give you what you cannot find in
yourself? And even if this person was
perfect, would you, feeling imperfect,
be able to accept what they offer?
Would you feel you <u>deserved</u> it?

We're O.K.!

I'M O.K.

I'M O.K.

Caring for yourself, providing for your own needs, having respect for yourself, and nurturing yourself means that you are capable of accepting good things for yourself, including the love of another. But you do not <u>rely</u> on anyone or anything to feel complete. You, alone, are enough.

 TWO HALVES DON'T MAKE A WHOLE...

 ...THEY MAKE A HOLE!

 Well, what's the point of relationships if we're supposed to be so together that we don't NEED anyone?

Well, few of us are complete enough to sit on a mountain alone, contemplating the Universe.

So another person comes into your life and suddenly you're on a crash course into all your blocks and resistances and ITs, things that prevent you from being complete. This person is your mirror. Why not learn from this? Now you know what you need to change!

 Nice navel

Taking care of yourself does not mean doing it all alone. A major part of your relationship with yourself <u>is</u> in your interactions with others. An intimate relationship is the arena for a full expression of yourself. It teaches you about YOUR ability to trust, forgive, be flexible, allow space. It also teaches you about YOUR sticky ITs, such as anger, fear, jealousy, expectations and possessiveness.

Caring for yourself means recognising that these blocks hold you back from feeling good about YOURSELF, from being complete.

2. FIX-IT IT

Wanting to change someone means that we have not taken on <u>that</u> person, but a <u>potential</u> person.

Do you love this person, or your <u>idea</u> of how this person <u>should</u> be, to suit YOUR needs?

To accept someone AS THEY ARE is to not expect them to change ONE THING!

He'd be all right if he drove a good car, wore black, spoke properly & liked Cajun food! But how would you recognise him?

BASICALLY... WHAT YOU SEE IS WHAT YOU GET!

But you knew I was a clown when you met me!

This person got on fine till you came along. They have their own reasons for doing things in a particular way, just as you have.

How do you know what's best for the other person? Is it best for <u>them</u> or best for <u>you</u>?

<u>Respect</u> the differences! Praise the things that you enjoy! By focussing on the good things, the rest will not be a problem.

Of course, you might <u>invite</u> someone to adapt their behaviour if it is causing you problems. They may agree to, or they may not. If it's in <u>their</u> best interests to change, they may decide to.

But laying down **ULTIMATUMS** is a way of bullying someone to comply with your rules. Even if you manage to get what you want this way are you

I hate the theatre, but I'll go!   Well it's time we had fun!

really getting FREE WILL or someone reacting from a FEAR OF LOSS? In this situation, even if you WIN, you LOSE.

3. TELEPATHIC IT

There is, however, a vast difference between demanding something of another person to meet your needs and taking the responsibility for meeting those needs yourself.

Ironically, part of meeting those needs may involve that other person.

The key here is in <u>expressing</u> your needs, without leaving it up to the person to guess what they are.

Say you're feeling a bit low but your partner is going out with friends. Rather than feel put out that you're alone, he doesn't care, tell him how you feel!

You are asking for what you want, without relying on telepathy. You are taking responsibility for your feelings by <u>communicating</u> them.

Your partner now knows how you feel. The air is cleared. He/she may or may not be able (or willing) to give you what you want, but the important thing is that you have been direct about your needs, without sending out blurred unspoken signals, which may be confusing or may have you feeling unnecessarily sulky or resentful.

4. POSSESSIVE IT

Loving someone surely means wanting the best for them, as you would for yourself, wanting them to grow, follow their own path and evolve into the best person they can be.

Mine, mine, mine!

The best for <u>them</u>, however, may not always be what YOU would choose.

Now, here's a tough question:
WHAT IF THE BEST FOR THAT PERSON WAS

LEAVING YOU?!

It is easy to let go of the things we don't really care about — a car, a job — but a significant person . . . ?

Well, look at it this way...

You and the person you're with were travelling on two different roads that have now intersected. For <u>now</u>, you're on the same track. Notice, however, that as you proceed, the scenery is constantly changing, and the road twists and turns, obscuring what's ahead. There may be another intersection, which takes your friend one way, while your track goes the other way. You have a choice:

(A) Wish them the best of journeys and let them go (even though sadly); OR

 **OR**

(B) Cling on, finding yourself away from your path in a land you have no place in.

If you are walking with someone now, make that enough.
You have no claims on this person, nor do they on you.
You have <u>chosen</u> to be travelling companions FOR NOW.

LET GO of creating roles for your partner
as the ONE and ONLY, the LAST LOVE, the SOULMATE.

WHY? Because these concepts set up expectations.
Without having to be ALL to another, you can make mistakes,
you can explore yourself, you don't <u>have</u> to be there forever
(though you may choose to be).

SO: WHAT IF LOVING SOMEONE MEANT FINDING:

This is how LOVING I can be
This is how FLEXIBLE I can be
This is how PATIENT I can be
This is how GENTLE I can be
This is how FORGIVING I can be

and This is how much I can LET GO ?

SO: The **IT BUSTERS!** for LOVE are:

AFFIRMATIONS AND VISUALISATION   to promote   **SELF-LOVE**

The more nurturing, support and love you are able to give to yourself, the less you will rely on others to provide it. A further bonus is that the more you can accept yourself as <u>worthy</u> of love, the easier it will be to receive and give it. Self-love makes you more appealing, too. Winners are attractive.

HOW, NOW?

Let the future unfold as it will. Enjoy your time with this person right now. Learn from them, grow with them. Love them for who they are, not who they <u>might</u> be.

RESPONSIBILITY

Own your <u>own</u> thoughts, words and deeds, not someone else's.
Appreciate the uniqueness of your partner.
If the differences are too great . . . you have CHOICE.

LETTING GO

The person you are with had a life before you. The things they need to do for themselves are still important. Give them (and yourself) space. Nothing grows in a suffocating environment.
Let go of demands and expectations.
<u>Share</u> your <u>individual</u> lives.
Relationship does not mean OWNERSHIP.

BEST for yourself is the BEST for everyone, because you are being TRUE to yourself.

FIT IT

Part of getting yourself whole again is to think of yourself as the <u>whole</u> person — MIND, BODY and SPIRIT.

A great deal of the work you've already done with IT has been about changing your thinking, and that new thinking is about CHOICE, about making the best and healthiest choices for yourself. So, in health, the best choices may include:

THE BEST THOUGHTS
THE BEST PHYSICAL CONDITION
and THE BEST BELIEFS.

MIND

The idea here is to think of the mind as consuming whatever you feed it, digesting this and producing the appropriate emotional response.

SO: If you feed the mind junk (negative thoughts), you'll feel bad. Conversely, feed the mind healthy ideas, and you'll feel happier and more peaceful.

As we have seen, affirmations and visualisation can help greatly in giving yourself the right brain food. Another important part of digestion is rest, to allow the mind to quieten and, therefore, the body and emotions to quieten too.

This is where meditation comes in.

Some people think of meditation as an exotic, foreign practice performed only by mystics and yogis who have little involvement in the rigours of everyday life.

Well, if you have ever gazed into a log fire and become mesmerised by the flames, then you have meditated. Can you recall that feeling? How time slipped away? How you did not <u>feel</u> anything, particularly? How it seemed as if all thought had stopped?

OMMM

A definition of meditation could be 'focussed attention'. Say you were seated on a riverbank watching the play of light on the water. Your <u>focus</u> had turned to the light on the water.

Your <u>attention</u> was on that one thing.

The word 'attention' is important. Rather than concentrating, which suggests forcing thought in a particular direction, with attention you are simply attending or witnessing, while your mind floats where it will, unencumbered by the travelogue we usually impose upon it. So, by <u>focussing</u> on the water, you are stilling your mind. No conclusions need to be reached. The exercise is complete in itself, there is no impingement of time, and there you are, just BEING. You are meditating.

Why are there Meditation Classes, then?

Because we are not used to 'turning inward' for our sense of wellbeing, and we are equally not used to the experience of just 'being', perfectly still, in one spot for up to an hour. A class will give you techniques for relaxing quickly, and a group situation increases the incentive to stay focussed and still until it becomes more natural to you. Many courses are available at low cost or free. When you start meditating, you might notice:

1. PHYSICAL DISCOMFORT

In your first sessions you may be extra aware of every little itch, twinge and ache. The thought of sitting still for a long period might get at you at first. Use your IT techniques — quietly allow the sensations and thoughts to be. Continue to relax into them, then LET THEM GO.

2. EXPECTATIONS

Expect nothing! Except, that is, a sense of calm and wellbeing afterwards. The idea is not to <u>strive</u> for anything, but to just be with the experience of yourself in a deeply relaxed state. Let any thoughts that want to come up, simply rise to the surface like bubbles, then drift away. No conclusions are necessary, just let thoughts come and go by being <u>detached</u> from them.

Meditation teaches those of us with anxiety an important thing: deep inside is actually a SAFE PLACE! Deep inside you is a sanctuary! IT cannot touch you there!

You may even hear his grumblings on the way down into relaxation and the thought may occur to you of just how noisy and restless IT is, compared to YOU!

You can learn to 'tune out' in many situations. Try it in a queue at the supermarket, instead of getting angry!

AND: Guided meditation tapes use affirmations and visualisation to help with problems.

BODY

Just as what we feed our mind influences our emotions, then what we feed our body influences how we handle those emotions.

People with anxiety are fairly sensitised to even minor physical shifts, and STIMULANTS can trigger symptoms very similar to those experienced during panic or anxiety. Stimulants include:

Coffee & Tea

Cola

Alcohol
(especially when it wears off)

Chocolate

Here are some more guidelines:

1. Steer clear of the above stimulants. Try herbal tea or coffee substitutes. 1 glass of beer or wine with a meal no more than 3–4 times a month (sorry!).

2. Avoid refined carbohydrates or sugars (white flour, pasta, bread, sugar, etc). These foods can cause low blood sugar, which can create anxiety symptoms. Particularly avoid them on an empty stomach. Choose whole grain instead.

3. Eat 3 moderate, balanced meals a day. Avoid snacking and overeating.

4. Increase low-fat dairy products. Tuna, turkey, lamb and liver are also helpful. And LOTS of fruit and vegies!

5. Avoid artificial sweeteners — they rev you up!

6. Avoid overly rich and spicy foods, for the same reason.

NATURAL HEALTH PRACTICES

There is currently a huge interest in natural forms of medicine and a wide range to choose from.

All tend to work from the idea that illness of any kind arises from energy blocks in the body, and, if you release these blocks, energy can begin to flow freely through the body, allowing healing to occur.

Because these blocks may have been long term, and deep-seated emotionally, the process of natural healing is a slower one than we are used to in more conventional medicine, and several regular visits may be required before any significant improvement occurs.

Natural medicine recognises the strong links between the emotional, mental and physical. It treats the whole person (using the 'holistic' approach) as the source of all illness. The release of deeper emotional issues following treatment can feel like a step back into the problem, but this tends to pass quickly. The whole treatment is based on <u>release</u> and <u>freeing up</u> the problem.

Therapeutic massage, acupuncture, kinesiology, shiatsu and naturopathy are a few of the disciplines reputed to be helpful for anxiety. Along with these, of course, is counselling, as we discussed more fully in *Living with IT*.

Your new thinking will greatly help the healing process, too, as you take more responsibility for your own recovery and health.

EXERCISE

Forget the schedules, the bulge-revealing gear, the pump and grind (unless you're into that already!). Take a hike!

A brisk walk for ½–1 hour a day will provide you with an outlet for physical and emotional stress AND you'll get fit, raising your self-esteem at the same time!

Walking is a means of low impact, aerobic exercise which can be worked into even the busiest schedule and it's FREE!

Some form of exercise is very important for IT sufferers, as anxiety tends to 'freeze' you into tight, inward postures, and you also tend to get 'stuck' in your own head.

Broad, expansive movements such as walking will help to 'open' you up, and the soothing effects of nature cannot be overstated in terms of helping to calm you mentally.
So, all you need is good shoes, some time and a patch of ground! Just do it!

PAIN

Pain is really a physical IT. The more you resent it, resist it and fight against it, the more hold it has over you. The same IT principles of shifting focus, self-talk, letting go and positive thinking apply to pain. Pain (and, indeed, other illness) is also trying to tell you something. Take note of the site of the pain. If we acknowledge that illness has an emotional origin, then we can <u>do</u> something about our own health. Many of the cliches in common use are actually quite revealing in this regard: 'I can't stomach it', 'It's a pain in the neck', 'Get it off your chest' etc may provide clues to emotional causes for our complaints.

Anxiety, for example, may be about not trusting life: not going with the flow, or needing to CONTROL things to feel safe.

Meditation can help with pain.
Try this: close your eyes
and go to the pain.
Study it in great detail.

What shape is it?
What size?
What colour?

Once you have a clear picture of the pain, gather it all up into a ball. Now imagine the ball getting smaller and smaller till it is the size of a pin head. Move the tiny ball down to your finger (or toe, depending on where it is to start with) and let it pop out of the end and disappear.

BAD DAYS

No matter how together you are, no matter how hard you have worked on yourself, there are going to be days when you wouldn't know a positive thought if you fell over it!

The temptation is to forget all of the times when you <u>have</u> been on top, <u>have</u> been able to turn things around and <u>have</u> felt good.

Well, if you can summon just <u>one</u> thought that will help you through, it's this: 'I'm having one of THOSE days. I'm not going to fight it, I'm going to go with it, all the way. I'm giving myself permission to feel BLEAAAGH till it passes.'

Then do whatever you need to do. Wallow in it. Indulge yourself. Make no apologies.

You'll feel better tomorrow,
or the next day. It's OK.

SPIRIT

What is 'SPIRIT'?

You vill meet a tall, dark stranger

Most people tend to link the word 'spirit' with the occult, or religion, but outside of your intellect and your physical being, there is another kind of self — the 'spirit' of who you are.

This self is part of what makes you who you are: unique and special. It is that quality of a person that we sense, or an atmosphere around a place that we pick up on. Regardless of what you call it, there is a part of you that has been deeply wounded by the past, and particularly by IT, a part which needs healing just as much as your mind or body. But how?

Well, what if you had a guidebook for living that gave you a set of ideals to work towards?

What if you knew what was required of you in ANY given situation? Would that make it all easier?

What if we conceded that, so far, we haven't done too well at running our lives (or the planet, for that matter) in the old way, and that maybe our spiritual selves — the essence of who we are, our purpose in life — needed a rethink as much as anything else? Of course, you have a CHOICE as to whether you aim for these ideals or not, but it might be worth noting that the more you do, the better you'll feel. Here they are:

1. Operate from a more loving perspective.

2. Live in the moment.

3. Get out of your HEAD and into your HEART.

4. What YOU do affects EVERYTHING, so do it right.

5. Go with the flow.

6. Believe in abundance, not limitation.

7. Accept responsibility for your WHOLE self.

LET'S TAKE A CLOSER LOOK:

1.  is not for the faint-hearted. Real love is not about sugary Valentine's card sentimentality, but about <u>really</u> caring about yourself, others and life, WITHOUT CONDITIONS. REAL love is just that: no games, no illusions, no manipulations, no tricks, no judgement, no envy.

This is NOT love:

I'll love you if you're good!

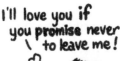

I'll love you if you promise never to leave me!

I'll love you if you lose 9 kilos!

And neither is this!

I'll love you if you're nice & never make mistakes or get angry or scared or get wrinkles or...

♪ ♪ I'm NOTHING without you ♪ & I'm a SHELL I'm LOST... ♪

I wish I had her looks!

119

To love

YOURSELF means: Acceptance of yourself as you are —
ALL of you, not just the 'nice' you.

OTHERS means: Acceptance, forgiveness, respect
and understanding. Not just words!

LIFE means: Respect for the planet, for all living
things and <u>gratitude</u> for life itself.

If you need a guideline, ask yourself this:

"What would be the LOVING thing to do?"

Love is not one-sided. You give it, you get it back.
You don't give it, well . . .
Try <u>caring</u> about everyone you meet and everything you do for
<u>1 week</u>. Just try it and watch what happens!

2. LIVING NOW As we saw in IT
Busters, make the present your whole
experience.
Forget the 'if onlys' and 'what ifs'!

3. HEAD TO HEART Call it intuition, gut instinct, insight,
there's a part of you that <u>knows</u> what to do. The easiest way to
know if you're listening to your heart
is that it will <u>feel</u> right or true. Your
head may not <u>like</u> what it hears, of
course, but it's YOUR truth, so be
<u>real</u> enough to listen to it.

← EEK!

← AHA!

This works with others, too. By getting out of your head and
into your heart, you may pick up on what is going on behind a
person's words. They may be lonely, or hurt.

4. DO IT RIGHT Ever noticed how one person's mood can affect a whole group?

What if I'm nasty to you? You're not going to feel good, so you're less likely to be nice to the next person, and so on. So, a ripple effect is created that goes on and on.

What you do, even how you treat others and the environment, affects EVERYTHING. You're actually very powerful! Better choose the best!

5. GO WITH THE FLOW No matter how much we resist, change is inevitable. You can either go with it, or get swamped by it. Open up to new experience. Trust the process of change.

6. ABUNDANCE We believe that things like love, money, happiness, and peace (for example) are LIMITED. We insure, protect, guard and cling onto what we do have, believing in its loss! We squeeze all the joy out of <u>having</u> love, money (and so on) by worrying about not having it any more! What if we <u>didn't</u> believe that these things were limited?

7. WHOLE SELF To be <u>aware</u> is to be authentic. This means being open to the FULL experience of you, and <u>valuing</u> each part equally. Without our downs, there'd be no ups!
FEEL IT ALL!
OWN IT ALL! It's who you ARE!

WHAT IF...

* You were <u>exactly</u> where you needed to be NOW to learn enough to move on?
* Everything was going to plan?
* IT was neither good nor bad, but an important experience?

* By going through this pain you found a better, wiser, more peaceful you than ever before?
* You gave in and let the Universe run you for a while, going along with <u>whatever</u> comes?

Wouldn't all this mean you could RELAX? Nothing more is required of you than that you experience this, learn from it and get it over with! No more victim mentality (why me?). Doesn't that take the pressure off?

HOW? Because you now have a CONTEXT for IT. You now have a <u>reason</u> for your pain. You now know what is required of you!

So, start working, <u>really working</u> to be whole again.

GROW, LEARN, BE THE BEST!

SO: Here's a daily set of practices that you could do for MIND, BODY and SPIRIT.

Affirmations

15 minutes or several times during the day

Meditation

½ hr morning or evening by yourself for yourself

Visualisation

While meditating or as required for a tricky situation

Pampering

A massage or neck rub (if available)

Walking

½–1 hr brisk walk morning or evening

Eating

Healthy food in 3 moderate meals a day (avoid stimulants)

SPIRIT:

DON'T FRET ~ Accept

Meditation will help here, too.

LOVE

For YOU
For OTHERS
For LIFE
Get it right
and you
won't need
this book!

Know it
Feel it
Try it
Use it
Give it
Receive it

Value all life
and all living
things

Embrace
ALL of your
experiences

Go with the flow
Go with change

Be able to say at the
end of the day 'I have
done no harm, to
myself, others or my
world'.

Ask:

 What did I learn
today?

TRUST that all is well. Really!

THAT'S IT!

This is me...

... And this is **IT**

Boy, the battles we've had together! But, I'm grateful to IT. Yes, grateful. IT has given me:

Insomnia	Meditation
Pain	And a way to transform it
Self-pity	Self-worth
Terror	And a knowledge that I survived — I can do ANYTHING!
Palpitations	Knowing to slow down
A sense of loss	An ability to let go
Depression	An awareness of choice
Suffering	Greater compassion
Lovelessness	Love
Urgency	Patience
Chaos	Direction
Self-centredness	Self-awareness
A sense of abandonment	A sense of trust
Unrest	Peace
Negativity	A new perception
Lack of focus	Commitment
Indecision	Resolution

PLUS: 2 books, and a chance to talk to YOU!

Some days he catches me off guard . . .

. . . but I've learned how to keep him in line, sometimes more easily than others, because I'm still learning.

And then it's time to really listen for what IT's telling me . . .
. . . about what I'm doing
. . . about where I'm at.

SO . . . IT is my teacher.

I can't say this will ever be a love affair . . .

but . . . who knows?
We've come a long, long way together, after all.
We're quite a team, really.

In fact, WHERE would I have been without him?

Probably not...

LIVING IT UP!!

LETTING IT GO

ATTAINING AWARENESS OUT OF **ADVERSITY**

Bev Aisbett

Dedicated,
with love,
to Buzzy
for being there in the dawn
that made the darkness all
worthwhile

AND
Deepest thanks for love, friendship,
support & gentle guidance, to
Robbi Zeck, David Milligan
and all at IVI

FOREWORD

Writing the `IT Books', as I fondly refer to them, has offered me great rewards:

- firstly, the privilege of seeing my own creativity immortalised;
- secondly, being in a position to offer hope and help to others through passing on all that I have learned – a great reward indeed;
- and thirdly, to see before me the very evidence of my own evolutionary course of discovery that began with survival, moved through understanding and has now embarked onto insight.

None of these gifts would have come my way if I had not had an **IT**, if I had not experienced what I saw at the time as great suffering.

It was through this very suffering that I was forced to face the fears that I could no longer ignore, work at the resistances I held, clear the blocks that stood in my way and heal the wounds that caused me such pain.

And, as a result, a profound change occurred. I became more aware, more conscious, more enlightened than I had ever been before.

In my quest to overcome what seemed to be an enormous obstacle, I was given the opportunity and the motivation to **change** the way I **lived**.

And so, I once again pass on to you all that I have discovered, in the hope that you too, may find your own answers and finally, peacefully, joyfully, let **IT** go.

Bev Aisbett

CONTENTS

A SPECIAL NOTE
FOR READERS
WITHOUT
PANIC PROBLEMS

The fact that you have not suffered severe anxiety,
depression or any other major emotional crisis, does not
exclude you from benefiting greatly from the information
and exercises contained in this and the two previous books.

Few of us go through life without *some* form of **IT**,
whether **IT** be addiction, dependence, illness, anger,
impatience, intolerance or one of a myriad other
problems around self-worth that hold us back from a true
expression of self, or a greater freedom to participate fully
and joyfully in life.

Someone suffering from extreme anxiety does not
necessarily need to change and grow to any greater degree
than many others - the need is just more *urgent*.

I invite you to follow the lead of those wonderful
panic people who, in courageously facing their fears
and blocks, have worked to rebuild their lives, not only
to ensure recovery from anxiety, but to become more
loving, independent, compassionate and responsible
citizens of the world.

Thank you

THE LAST IT BITS

Where are you now?

So, **IT**'s still around, eh?

But boy, hasn't he changed!

He's gone from *this* ...   to *this* ...

... or even *this*!

IT has evolved from being a major obstacle to become an occasional **annoyance** or, hopefully, **a tool for growth**! And it's all through *your* hard work!!

CONGRATULATIONS!

Look how far you've come!

You've gone from being **overwhelmed** by **IT** ...

... to living with **IT**!

In order to achieve this, you took back control by ...

- accepting ownership of your **IT**

- recognising self-defeating patterns in your thinking

- monitoring and halting negative self-talk

- realising that fear did not stop you from functioning.

And, having completed your work in these areas, you moved on to ...

... living **IT** up!

This meant ...

- recognising **IT** in all of **IT's** forms - anger, guilt, self pity - anything that stood in the way of your enjoyment of life

- seeing **IT** as a barometer for the blocks that need work

- not resisting **IT** but working *with* **IT** to instigate positive changes.

And, if you *have* done your homework, by now you probably will have developed ...

- greater self-worth
- a more flexible attitude to life's changes

- more positive self-supporting life choices
- a greater acceptance of others and self
- an increased ability to live in the present.

If not ... sorry, roll up those sleeves and keep working at it!

(I *never* said it was **easy**!!)

Here's a **before** and **after** comparison. These are the changes you might have made to your thinking by now. How do you rate?

BEFORE IT

AFTER IT

I should have done better!
I musn't be late!
I can't do that!

I gave it my best shot!
I'll get there when I can!
I could try and see!

NOW! Rigid, limiting words seldom (if ever!) appear in your vocabulary. You are conscious of the words you choose.

You're wrong!

Well, I see it differently!

NOW! In a conflict situation, you take responsibility for **your** position only and choose 'I' statements instead of levelling blame and criticism at others.

Oh no! Another disaster! This is too much! I can't cope!

Hmm... how can I fix this? Where am I stuck?

NOW! You've stopped fretting, complaining and dramatising about your problems. When you encounter a problem, you get on with seeking a solution.

BEFORE IT   # AFTER IT

You look nice!

What? My hair's a mess, I've put on weight...

I like your outfit!

Thank you!

NOW! You've stopped negating, apologising for, **comparing** and **putting down** yourself (and others).

Just my luck to be stuck in this job! I wish I was out of here!

I'm going to write to other companies!

NOW! You've stopped blaming luck, God, fate or others for your problems. You take **active steps** to improve your situation instead of wishing problems would magically disappear by themselves.

AND...

By **NOW!** quite simply, you feel **better**!

13

If even **half** of these improvements are in place, then surely **IT** has served a **positive** function!

IT has given you the **incentive** to make the changes necessary to give you a **better outlook on life!**

BLEAGH
HATE
RUSH
FEAR
WORRY
RESENT
FRET
GUILT
ANGST INC

Think back. Remember how
NEGATIVE
you were?
How weighed down by
pain, worry, fear, anger
and trouble?

Can you honestly say that, without **IT**, you would have put in the **effort** required to turn all that around?

But **IT**s work is now over. It's time for ...

LETTING IT GO!

Thanks for the lesson! BYEEE!

Hurrumph!. I know when I'm not wanted!

And this involves ...

- understanding where **IT** began
- seeing the **BIG PICTURE** of your struggle
- making peace with the past
- developing a loving attitude
- releasing fear, anger and negativity
- becoming more focused and conscious
- trusting your own wisdom
- living in the present.

In order to do this, you will need to **really work** at the following:

1 HONESTY

The first key to freedom is in being **honest** with yourself. **Really honest.** To effectively remove the cheap drama from your life, you will need to identify when **you** are playing a part in it and face that.

To have **trust** in yourself, you will need to know that you do not rely on **tricks** to get by. This requires courage.

2 IDENTIFYING YOUR BLOCKS

You are a whole human being. Your responses, reactions and resistances have an impact on **all** areas of your life, including your health and your circumstances. Identifying and taking responsibility for your blocks will give you valuable insights for growth.

3 GETTING OUT OF YOUR COMFORT ZONES

To fully free yourself, you will need to be prepared to address your fears, anger, blocks and resistances. This can be painful, especially as they become more obvious the more you work at clearing them. But the pay-off is worth it. No pain - no gain! How **much** are you prepared to do to feel better?

4 PATIENCE AND PERSEVERANCE

And all of this will require that you hang in there! **Half** a commitment to success will only give you half-baked results! Many people stop short just when they are on the verge of **BREAKING THROUGH**! Stay with it!

So, let's begin with honesty, and take a look at where you are now.

Complete this questionnaire by filling in the percentage.

		% YES	% NO
I AM WHERE I WANT TO BE IN:	■ My work		
	■ My homelife		
	■ Relationships		
I FEEL NURTURED AND SUPPORTED BY:	■ My friends		
	■ My family		
	■ My partner		
	■ My workmates		
WHEN DEALING WITH OTHERS, I FEEL MOSTLY:	■ Intimidated		
	■ Defensive		
	■ Judgemental		
	■ Equal		
	■ Superior		
	■ Inferior		
I HAVE IDENTIFIED MY LIFE'S PURPOSE			
I ASK FOR WHAT I WANT WITHOUT USING :	■ Charm		
	■ Ultimatum		
	■ Helplessness		
	■ Hints		
	■ Threats		
	■ Put-downs		
IF SOMEONE HAS SUCCESS, I FEEL:	■ Happy		
	■ Envious		
	■ Competitive		
	■ Resentful		
	■ Sorry for self		
IF SOMEONE NEEDS HELP, I AM LIKELY TO:	■ Educate them		
	■ Rescue them		
	■ Give advice		
	■ Ask what they need		
	■ Retreat		

I TRY TO CHANGE OTHERS

I LIVE IN THE PAST

I SEE PROBLEMS AS:
- *Challenges needing solutions*
- *Punishments*
- *My bad luck*
- *Opportunities*

I AM EASILY ABLE TO FORGIVE PERCEIVED SLIGHTS

I FEEL HARD DONE BY

PEOPLE UNDERSTAND ME

I RELY ON OTHERS' OPINION OF ME TO FORMULATE MY OWN OPINION OF SELF

I OFTEN CRITICISE:
- *Others*
- *Authorities*
- *Myself*

I GIVE MORE THAN I GET BACK

MY OWN JUDGEMENT IS TRUSTWORTHY

I WOULD RATHER BE ALONE THAN IN A RELATIONSHIP THAT IS NOT ABSOLUTELY 50/50

I CAN GET ALL THE SUPPORT, NURTURING, ATTENTION AND LOVE I NEED WITHOUT
- *Struggle*
- *IT*
- *Ill health*
- *Addiction*
- *Being perfect*
- *Being indispensible*
- *Being dependent*
- *Being special*

I LIKE WHO I AM AND WOULD NOT WANT TO BE ANYONE ELSE

Thank you. Your answers will reveal the areas you need to work on.

17

OK, on the following pages we will begin working towards letting **IT** go.

In order to proceed, I would now like to introduce you to some exciting **POSSIBILITIES**!

This will require you to open up to some **NEW THINKING**, but, hey, you've already done a lot of that by now, haven't you?

No matter how unfamiliar this may seem, I can **GUARANTEE** you this...that if you begin to live out these possibilities, you **WILL** feel better! Worth a try, eh?

Here they are ...

- The purpose of this physical experience – life – is to **learn**. It's *supposed* to be challenging!
- All events have a purpose. Everything has a reason.
- All the wisdom, peace, strength and love you need is already inside you.
- You are not given more than you can handle(!).
- A painful situation or pattern will repeat until it is resolved and cleared.
- Each of us is working from a different script, but working towards the same goal.
- All suffering arises from our own attitude to suffering.
- Wisdom cannot be achieved by an intellectual exercise alone. It can only come from **experience**.
- Your body is no more than a vehicle for **YOU**.
- Everything is connected. Anything is possible.
- What you **believe** will happen, probably will.
- Love is an antidote to all suffering.

BELIEVE IT OR NOT?

The role of a belief system in recovery

The pioneer of psychology, Carl Jung, made an interesting observation. People under his care who had a **spiritual context** to their lives were more likely to experience recovery from emotional breakdown than those who didn't. Why would this be so?

The dictionary defines `spirit' as `the force or principle of life that animates the body of living things'.

So, one might surmise that to have a `spiritual context' in one's life would be to have a meaning for life based on the existence of this greater force.

How might this be helpful to someone suffering from, say, anxiety or depression?

In times of distress particularly, we search for a meaning for our suffering.

We look for a source of help in dealing with our problems. We reach out for comfort and understanding.

Without a reason for our distress, we feel stuck, lost, powerless and unable to move on.

There seems to be no pattern or logic to the events in our lives. We stumble along, hoping for the best, but fearing the worst.

When 'bad' things happen to us, we tend to allocate responsibility for our hardship in one of the following ways ...

1 OURSELVES
We either take responsibility or bear the burden of blame.

2 OTHERS
We allocate blame outside ourselves, because we don't have to face or solve a problem we don't *own*.

3 DIVINE JUDGEMENT
We perceive we are being rewarded or punished for our virtues or sins accordingly.

4 LUCK
We attribute events and circumstances to chance - no one's responsibility and no control, either.

And, whether you feel safe or vulnerable, judged or accepted, and whether the Universe is a friendly or hostile place for you, will be governed by your **spiritual view**, and this, in turn, will have been highly influenced by your conditioning and upbringing. Let's take the idea of God, for instance.

For you, God may be ...

A PARENT

As a **parent**, God may be loving or punishing, reflecting your own parents' behaviour towards you when you were growing up.

AN AUTHORITY FIGURE

Vengeful or rewarding, capricious or supportive, depending on your experience of higher authorities, this idea of God will set the rules and operate as a governing force to be feared and revered.

This idea of God will again reflect how much nurture and support you received. This God may not be there for you when you need Him, or may not exist at all for you.

ABSENT

Or, God may be more abstract for you ...
- a Divine Energy
- a Transcendental Force
- a Natural Order.

All of this will affect your world view and your sense of worth and safety.

BASICALLY—

If you have high self-esteem you are more likely to perceive a safe Universe governed by a loving force.

If your self-esteem is low the Universe will feel threatening and you will anticipate punishment for mistakes.

So, we can see from this that an individual's spirituality and psychology are so closely linked as to be two sides of the same coin.

And, given this, your idea of **spirituality** will also be highly coloured by your **experience** of **religion** in your upbringing.

 But aren't **RELIGION** and **SPIRITUALITY** one and the same?

Not really. Let's turn to the dictionary again for a definition of `religion'.

RELIGION: `A formal or institutionalised expression of belief in divine powers.'

Religion involves a set of **rituals** and **practices** that **connect** us to the **spiritual.**

 OMM...

So, it could be argued that **spirit**, this `force', exists, whether we practice **religion** (i.e. connect with it) or not!

In fact, many people have become disillusioned by the conventional Church. Here are some of their views:

 I always leave church feeling guilty-like. I'm a sinner. I don't feel good about myself!

 I can't figure out how we can kill others in the name of God! It's hypocritical!

 The idea of a loving God doling out eternal punishment doesn't make sense!

 People in my religion seem to feel theirs is the only way and that others are wrong. Isn't that judgmental?

 If I'm such a **hopeless sinner**, I'll probably end up **damned**. If so, how can I feel **good** about life?

 My mother used to say 'God will get you for this!' Religion meant fear and guilt for me!

23

We turn to religion, or a belief system, to find a purpose for our lives, a reason for our suffering, as well as a hope for the future.

If the belief system you have adopted does not satisfy these criteria, does not leave you feeling supported and nurtured, then perhaps your *beliefs* need to be re-examined.

ABOUT BELIEFS

Back to the dictionary again.
To `believe' is `to *accept as true ... to think, assume, suppose.'*

Our *beliefs* can be erroneous.

You're a DUD!
You're STUPID!
You'll never get rid of me!

You believed all the stuff **IT** told you didn't you?

We all **BELIEVED** the Earth was **FLAT**, didn't we?

So, how were these **beliefs** changed?

WE EXPERIENCED OTHERWISE!

Here's Fred – Women are inferior to men!

and here's Harry. – Women are our equals!

Both these men have **beliefs**. They arrived at their vastly different beliefs through different experiences and perceptions. For both Fred and Harry, this is the *truth*. For either to change their beliefs, they will need to experience otherwise, and in order to change, they will have to become dissatisfied with their current experience or transformed by a new experience.

Many people, having experienced a lack of fulfilment through the beliefs espoused by one religion, tend to turn their backs completely on the pursuit of *any* spiritual life.

What may need to be questioned, however, is not spirituality, per se, but rather, this one particular approach to it.

Cultures throughout the world adopt widely varying means to exploring and accessing a spiritual path, and the system you were brought up with is only *one* of them. The goal, however, remains the same - union with a Divine force, and as such, a return to our original perfection.

But whatever path you choose, your physical, mental and emotional life will be greatly enhanced by developing a spiritual outlook.

HOW? Well, let's look at what having a spiritual outlook might mean.

☆ We accept that the force that manages to keep a whole Universe in balance might just be better at running things than we are!

☆ We accept change, rather than permanence, as the natural way.

☆ We begin to move *with* change rather than insisting on our own desired outcomes.

☆ We stop labelling experiences as `good' or `bad', instead seeing each situation as part of the full experience of life.

☆ We recognise that the same energy that constitutes all of life, is not **outside** us, but is housed **within** us, connecting us to each other, and all living things.

Most major cultures employ metaphors, fables and myths to explain the workings of things and to simplify concepts. Here is a new one to help explain the above points and how you fit in ...

The Journey

There was (and still is) a vast, knowing, utterly balanced, perfect energy called **THE SOURCE**.

THE SOURCE contained all of the ingredients that were to become you and me, trees, cars, even nuclear bombs ... **everything**, but at this stage these things were just **possibilities**, for then **THE SOURCE** had no form. It was just pure energy, playing through space, and we were part of it.

And, because everything connected to **THE SOURCE** was in perfect balance, there was complete knowing and harmony ...

Then, one day the energy that was to

YAHOO!

become you and me, spotted something called the **physical plane**!

As part of **THE SOURCE**, we had free will, of course.

This is cool! — Yeah!

... But the only way to stay on the **physical plane** was to take to a **physical form** ...

Hey, great outfit!   Thanks! Yours too!

So we decided to explore this **physical plane**.
... Thereby removing ourselves from **THE SOURCE**!

And, of course, what we had chosen was **LIFE**, and *all* of its experiences ...

But by now, we had completely forgotten our **SOURCE**. We totally believed that we could control everything, and think and fight and invent our way out of this mess.

And so we trudged on, lifetime after lifetime, repeating the same mistakes, until, finally, we caught a glimpse of what we'd had all along ...

All we had to do to reconnect with **THE SOURCE** was to **remember** its energy was within us, but we soon forgot. We decided we knew better. After all, we had **free will**, and this was our choice.

JOY   SORROW   PAIN   SEX

FEAR   HATRED   LOVE   AND DEATH

Soon, we discovered that, though the good bits of life were great, the bad bits could hurt us badly. We had trouble handling life.

We had forgotten how to connect with all the peace, balance, wisdom, strength and power we began with.

... and by clearing away all the negativity and illusion, we revealed a treasure that lay within us - **THE SOURCE** - our own true selves.

What could this mean to you?

Perhaps this is just a story. Or perhaps it's not!
Let's review some of the possibilities that appear on page 18.

- **LIFE IS EDUCATION.**
  LIFE IS CHALLENGING.

If we have lost sight of our original perfection, then we have to address our blocks to this perfection. This means pain whenever we hit those blocks. We will do this many times before learning to clear them. We're slow learners.

- **ALL YOU NEED IS INSIDE YOU.**

May **THE SOURCE** be with you!
   The same energy that makes the grass grow, the wind blow and the sun shine, makes you tick as well! You just need to learn how to *access* it! And, for every handicap you have, you possess a compensatory strength. Are you using it?

- **ALL EVENTS HAVE A PURPOSE.**

I need to learn patience!

Where you are at is exactly where you need to be to learn whatever you need to learn. Pain is a great motivator. Look back over your life. When did you learn the most? When you were happy or when you were challenged?

- **YOU ARE NOT GIVEN MORE THAN YOU CAN HANDLE.**

Feels that way! But the minute you *choose* to handle something, you do! We have **free will**.
   Some people survive hideous circumstances and come out smiling. Some people kill themselves over a broken love affair!
                    Choice.
You can go with it and grow. Give in and you'll never know.

- **A PAINFUL SITUATION WILL REPEAT TILL CLEARED.**

If you do what you've always done, you'll get what you've always got. Did you `get it' last time or just blunder back in and hope it will turn out better by doing the *same*? You are not being **punished**. You are being **educated**. Clear the block and move on.

- **SUFFERING IS AN ATTITUDE.**

There is no `punishment' or `reward'. `Punishment' arises from our own resistances and holding of pain. The `reward' comes from living *any* experience *well*. Life is not about `good' or `bad' experiences - just **contrasts**. We label experiences good or bad according to our **perception** of them. In fact, there is no prize, no goal to be reached! The journey ends where it began ... with your true self, until now buried under illusions and pain.

- **EACH OF US HAS A DIFFERENT SCRIPT.**

If we consider that we're all on a journey back to our perfection, then some people will be further along with their lessons than others. Don't judge! Someone may be figuring out raw physical strength, while someone else may be working on material or mental lessons. Their scripts are just *different* from yours, but no less (or more) valid.

- **WISDOM ONLY COMES FROM EXPERIENCE.**

Believing in a spiritual force is not as important as **opening** to it. A purely intellectual approach may give you ideas but only through direct experience will you gain **wisdom**. Listen - your heart's beating. Do you have to **believe** in it for it to do so? That's how it is with a spiritual energy. If you open to it, you'll experience it. And really, does it matter *where* healing comes from?

QUESTIONS

- Did you grow up in a religious environment?
- If you did, was it a spiritually nourishing environment?
- If you could picture a god, what would he/she/it look like?
- Where do you believe this god abides?
- Does giving a spiritual force a persona limit its power for you? Or enhance it?
- Do you believe in divine punishment or reward? Why?

EXERCISE

Close your eyes and try to picture yourself as pure energy, and your body as just the shell that contains it.

See yourself as an energy that is perfect – balanced, loving, peaceful, timeless, accepting, wise and calm.

Now picture yourself moving through life from this new viewpoint.

How differently would you feel, think or behave?

What would be your attitude towards your body in this context?

MY STORY

One day, during a particularly rough patch, when I was feeling pretty sorry for myself, I got thinking about the above idea. What if I was a spiritual being? How would I behave?

With this in mind, I went to the beach, and decided to try to operate from that level. I became very calm, a little aloof, very wise and dignified.

And suddenly, I also found I had a new appreciation of the water, the rocks, the sun and the air as being forms of energy that fed my own. I no longer felt so alone and powerless. I was part of it all, and everything was exactly as it needed to be.

THIS IS YOUR LIFE

The origins of low
self-esteem

So, this is the script you've been given for your journey.

It determines your character - your race, gender, personality, physical and mental qualities and all the challenges that go with these.

It contains many entrances and exits, cues and upstagings. You only receive one page at a time.

How well you perform this page will influence what follows.

And, for this particular drama, **IT** has been written into the script ...

For most of us, he starts out playing the

VILLAIN...

... but he has every chance of becoming the **HERO!**

Meanwhile, however, **IT's** part in the play brings you a challenging role, filled with ALL of life's great dramas ...

FEAR

ANGER

GUILT

ILL HEALTH

... to name but a few!

And at the bottom of these is one common thread ...

LOW SELF-ESTEEM!

Given that this play is all about working through your biggest lessons, we need to go back and find out where this low self-esteem came from and how it figures in the scheme of things.

In order to do this, let's meet the cast ...

THE EXTRAS ...   **... THE CAMEO ROLES**   **THE KEY PLAYERS**

These are the 1000s of nameless faces you encounter each day ...

... some of whom will move in and out of your life at a particular time and for a particular reason.

These include family, friends, partners, colleagues and authority figures.

All have a key role and all have been perfectly cast for this drama. Everyone's timing is impeccable, everyone says the right lines on cue, and everyone enters and exits exactly when they should.

And, of course, the STAR is...

- How will you go?
- Will you fulfil your role?
- Will you figure out the plot?

Let's see ...

CURTAIN UP!
APPLAUSE!
Let's begin!

SCENE 1 – YOUR ARRIVAL

Here you are, snuggly, floating in your mother's belly. You're perfect!!

Then, suddenly, you are catapulted out into the harsh glare of reality ...

... to meet your first key players (and role models) – your parents*.

(*or significant others – elders, authority figures, etc.)

Already, according to *your* script,
there may be snags ...

Your parents might be like this ...   ... or they might be like this!

The influence of your parents and other elders runs very
deep. What you learn from them in your developmental
years helps to form the patterns and responses of a lifetime.
They are your **role models.**
They give you your view of the world.

That the world is
wonderful and safe...

...or that the world is
corrupt ,evil and dangerous.

They show you what you
might expect from others ...

... and how to behave
towards them.

Support ... or betrayal   with cooperation   ... or contempt.

They give you examples of how **love** operates ...

that love
heals..

or love
hurts.

In other words...
they teach you how
to
"DO" LIFE!

 Before we get into **blaming** Mum and Dad ...

I did the best I could with what I had!

Remember that Mum and Dad had *their* scripts to work through too, which dictated *their* particular values and behaviour!

And so did I!

Be generous. What they began with may have been very limited indeed!

But whatever they were like, they were perfectly cast for you to learn what you most need to (as you will see)!

So according to everyone's **key players** and **role models,** things proceed to plan.

For a while, at least, everything may look rosy ...

You are the
CENTRE
of the
UNIVERSE!

All of your needs are met and all you have to do to get attention is *scream*!!
(Sound familiar?)

There is no question about your worth or lovability. You are perfect simply because you exist. You don't have to **please.** You are fully self-absorbed.

Then, as time goes by, you begin to become aware of the outside world and your unique place in it.

You start to become an **individual.**

This can be a rough transition.

For a start, you feel like **exploring** ...

... and for the first time you encounter the idea of being **wrong**.

The messages begin to become more and more mixed. You are compelled to explore this new world and your territory ... but this can bring trouble.

You begin to wonder if you can be yourself, be independent, be an individual ...

... and still be **loved**!

Just how tricky this transition is will depend on a lot of factors involving your parents.

• THEIR OWN SCRIPTS

Your parents inherited issues from *their* parents. Perhaps they had worked through these issues, perhaps not. Quite possibly, they had never even thought of having `issues', and so, in ignorance, the legacy goes on.

• HOW LOVING THEY WERE

Your parents may not have shown physical affection and you felt un-nurtured. They may have been violent and you felt unloved. Or they may have been so over-protective that you felt smothered.

• THEIR ATTITUDE TO DISCIPLINE

Again, this will have been greatly influenced, not only by how heavily disciplined they themselves were when growing up, but also by the popular thinking of the time.

In essence, the ease with which you evolved into your own person will have been affected by how many **rules** you had to live by in order to be accepted.

Scene 2 - Society

 But you may have been fortunate. Your script may have allowed for your earliest days to be filled with unconditional love and acceptance ...

 ... and full of confidence, you began to move out into the world ...

... only to discover that fitting into society added a whole new set of demands and restraints.

Aspects of your behaviour, once praised as lovable, suddenly became unacceptable ...

You were suddenly confronted with a confusing and conflicting set of messages that told you how to be, how to act and what to think.

... like showing your knickers ...

... or being too ` honest'

In order to be **accepted** you learned to **conform** ...

The message, loud and clear was ...

... and, in **conforming** you began to lose your spontaneity.

To fit in, you had to squash down what was once your natural expression of self. (And, to a child, even small things are significant.)

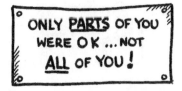

ONLY PARTS OF YOU WERE OK ... NOT ALL OF YOU!

By now, you will have had to do a lot of **improvising** to navigate this obstacle course into self-worth and self-reliance.

Other factors in your script will have also affected your degree of success in this. Some of these are:

• **YOUR PERSONALITY**   • **YOUR PHYSICAL APPEARANCE**

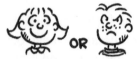

You may have an easy-going temperament and laugh off problems, or you may be very practical and able to reason your way through.

You may be sensitive and easily hurt. You may be led by your emotions.

Like it or not, our society worships physical beauty and bodily perfection. If you were at all `different' growing up, life would have been more challenging for you.

• **YOUR ENVIRONMENT**

Perhaps you came from a strict upbringing ...

... or a somewhat *laissez faire* environment.

There may have been cultural restrictions ...

Or generational differences ...

... or religious/political beliefs.

There may have been financial constraints ...

... or too much emphasis on power or material gain.

● **FAMILY HIERARCHY**

Depending on where you appeared in the pecking order, you may have encountered problems in your developmental years as a result.

 As a first-born, you may have become a junior parent, with responsibilities to your younger siblings.

The only child, growing up with adults, may miss out on developing self-reliance and independence, or become spoiled and self-indulgent.

 A middle child may find him/herself vying for attention between the eldest and youngest and feel left out.

 The 'baby' may remain that – gaining extra attention and expecting this outside the family.

All of these factors make growing into a healthy, balanced totally **OK** adult, at the very least, difficult, if not virtually impossible! No wonder we have **ITs**!

SCENE 3 – ENTER THE VILLAIN!

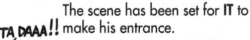

The scene has been set for **IT** to make his entrance.

Let's do one more flashback to your first days in the world.

You were complete. You responded naturally and instinctively. You experienced **wholeness**.

Then, as we saw, any love or acceptance that you received, started to have **conditions** on it.

I'll love you if you're good, don't cry, don't embarass me and behave by my rules!

In order to be **OK**, i.e. **acceptable**, certain natural behaviours and responses had to be **suppressed**.

For example:

Playing with yourself was no longer allowed – your natural sexuality was denied

Having a tantrum was not acceptable – your expression of anger was denied.

So, if you encountered a lot of rules in your formative years about what was acceptable and if your feelings were not acknowledged or allowed expression, more and more parts of you would have had to be disowned, in order for you to fit in. The things that you could no longer own became

The Buried Self

The **BURIED SELF** is like a cupboard into which we place certain thoughts, feelings and behaviours that are not approved of or encouraged.

Into this cupboard go natural behaviours we have to suppress, and with this goes our natural expression of self.

We also store away aptitudes that we have had to deny, and so we grow up believing that we can't achieve in certain areas - can't be strong, for instance, or are not good at sports, as another example, or can't draw, etc., because abilities were suppressed in these areas.

So, how does **IT** fit in here?

YUM! Well, inevitably, there will be times when you forget and do the very thing that is not allowed ...

WRONG!! When suddenly, you are aware of the voice of authority in your head, telling you this is **bad**!

BZZT! And with that comes a jolt of anxiety - enter **IT** stage left.

Too many of these and you begin to become anxious about doing *anything*.

You become afraid to **be yourself**. Being yourself **hurts**. You present a cardboard cut-out of yourself to the world – a false presentation of yourself that is acceptable to others.

This compensatory mask can have its own drawbacks. For instance:

 If your childhood lacked affection ...

... you may cut yourself off from the longing for affection by completely *rejecting* it ...

... and, as a result, you are perceived as someone who is cold, hard or aloof ...

... which can bring you even more hurt!

More and more goes into the cupboard as we struggle to fit in.

More and more we lose touch with our original wholeness.

It becomes harder and harder to contain these stored emotions and frustrations. It becomes harder and harder to maintain the false image that we have erected. Little bits begin to pop out, in tears, anger, resentment, and anxiety.

Eventually ...
we feel **bad** enough
to face the issue.

And it is at this point, that the true **HEALING** can begin.

QUESTIONS

- What do you think is the greatest lesson you need to learn from your life?
- What does your parents' example tell you about the way you live your life?
- If your parents are perfectly scripted to bring about necessary change in you, how so?
- Listen to your parent's voice in your head. What does it say?
- Do you have a dream? Are you working to fulfil it?

EXERCISE

Compile a list of your parents' better qualities and their shortcomings.

Now compile a list of your own.

In what ways do they match?

In what ways do they differ?

MY STORY

My parents had lost a daughter before I was born, and my mother was very ill when she was carrying me, to the degree that abortion was considered.

With only one sibling twelve years older than me, I grew up virtually as an only child surrounded by adults.

My struggle as an adult was to overcome dependency, not to fear solitude and to trust my own judgement.

I learned to hide these `shortcomings' by *appearing* to be strong-willed, direct and fiercely independent.

STUMBLING BLOCKS

Recognising blocks to recovery

To begin **HEALING**, we must first begin to recognise the **blocks** that stand in the way of this healing.

Doing this is similar to peeling away the layers of an onion, and can produce just as many tears in the process.

But what you are about to peel away, in this and the next few chapters, are all the layers of defence; the barricades that have kept you locked up in anxiety and frustration. The energy that it has taken to hold the **BURIED SELF** at bay has been enormous. Now you are ready to take the next step: the return to your true, whole self.

DON'T BE AFRAID TO FEEL

Keeping a lid on your emotions may have made you socially acceptable, but in so doing, you have created a pressure cooker inside. These feelings then tend to pop out in other ways - in grouchiness, tearfulness, resentment, and, of course, panic attacks!

The interesting thing is, these little outbursts alienate you even more!

So, our first efforts must be to identify these blocks and set about clearing them to allow true healing to occur.

It is time to tell the truth to yourself.

For years you have bought an image of yourself that has been distorted, as you will have seen by listening in to **IT**.

As a result, many of us are unfamiliar with who we really are, and by choosing to live with integrity, we must be prepared to shed light on the 'difficult' parts of ourselves.

Jung calls this part of ourselves that holds our fears and pain, '**THE SHADOW**'.

Walking *towards* the Shadow can lead to a difficult period, but great freedom lies beyond.

In your preparedness to live truthfully, it becomes harder to support the lies and deceptions of your old thinking, and as a result, a heightened awareness of these blocks throws them into stark relief.

This can sometimes be a humbling and somewhat painful experience.

But you are aiming to become more **ENLIGHTENED** and enlightenment means casting a **light on**, clearing out the dark spots within. Turn a light on and darkness disappears!

Enlightenment can also mean becoming **lighter**: less burdened and free of the baggage that has weighed you down for a lifetime, so that you can finally get on with **real** living!

Clearing out your blocks means being prepared to step out of your comfort zone in order to grow.

It means discovering ways of having *your* needs met, of nurturing *yourself*, of looking after *yourself*, by *yourself*. It means recognising that no one else can (or should) do this as well as *you* can!

So, let us begin, but first:

REMEMBER

This is not about YOU being unacceptable!
It is about the things that are STUCK being unacceptable.

Introducing~

The Catalogue

of

COMMON BLOCKS

PROJECTION

Whatever we can't tolerate inside, we tend to see outside. Projection such as this involves disowning our own feelings and placing them onto another. We do this not only with individuals, but with organisations, authority figures and objects: it's the car's fault, the boss's fault, the government's fault. This places the responsibility elsewhere and absolves us from our responsibility to own our anger, impatience, failings, etc.

HELPLESSNESS

Oh dear me! I could **never** do that! I need **you** to do it!

Are you playing the child?

In being helpless, inadequate or ineffectual, we give away our power. By getting someone else to take over, we don't even have to try!

It is up to **you** to instigate your own growth and healing. Part of this *may* involve recruiting the help of others – to help you to **help yourself**.

ORGANISING

Here, I'll do it!

Followed by ...

I have to do **everything!**

Many of us have a tendency to take over, then resent the extra burden of responsibility! Correcting this involves recognising that others are entitled to live their lives their own way, no matter how this clashes with *your* ideals! If you're into organising or `rescuing', recognise that you are removing another person's right and responsibility to sort out their own lives and make their own mistakes. How does it serve *you* to take over? Does it make you feel needed? Why do you only feel important doing it *this* way?

INVISIBILITY

No one listens to me!

If you are not being heard or your message is often misunderstood, what does that say about your communication?

- Do you **value** your opinions?
- Do you state your needs clearly or **hope** that people will `just know' what you want?
- Do you **speak up** if something bothers you?
- Do you **expect** to be heard?

DENIAL

It's not my fault!
She let me down!

This requires full ownership of *your* stuff.

You will need to recognise your own role in your present circumstances: your own reactions, blocks and limitations.

If you feel let down, put upon, ripped off etc., what part of you **allowed** this to happen?

MISERLINESS

Boy! She gets all the breaks! Why not me?

You think you've got it bad! Well, wait till you hear what happened to me!

How **excited** can you be for another person?
How much joy can you share without getting into *your own* stuff?
Similarly, how much can you give of yourself to another in their suffering without going 'one better' with *your* sad story? Learn to be generous with:

- your time
- your feelings
- your attention
- your deeds

You'll feel better!

MIND-READING

I know what you're thinking!

Actually, you **don't** know what another is thinking.
Ask, don't **assume**.

GIVING

I give and I give... what about me?!

Do you give till it hurts? Why? What if you stopped?

Giving is fine, if the motive is pure. Giving however, can be a device to receive attention, admiration, appreciation or affection in return, and this always backfires.
No one wants a gift with the price tag attached!

EXPECTATIONS

I expect you to be more considerate!

How **crowded** is your life with rules?

The only person you can make rules for is *you*. Having rigid rules for other people's behaviour will leave you constantly frustrated, because people will always deviate from them!

Allow things to unfold - let yourself be surprised by a different outcome to the one you were fixed on.

COERCION

You'll do that for little old me, won't you?

Surrendering this means being clear and direct in asking for what you want without resorting to charm, nagging, blaming, whingeing and sulking, etc. to receive it. **Ask for what** you need and **risk being refused.**

GUILT

Oh great! I do everything for you and you're too tired to help me!

Using guilt is another way of **blackmailing** to get what you want. You don't have to play that game! As above, be **direct** in your requests. Don't buy into other people's guilt either. Remind them of what they're doing, and refuse to be part of it.

REGRET

I wish I'd been more patient!

There's only one way to stop regretting, and that's to **stop doing the things that you'll regret**! What's done is done! Recognise the problem and **fix** it. Don't **agree** to something if you would rather **refuse** it!

PHYSICAL BLOCKS

Often our biggest blocks are apparent in the way that we present ourselves to the world. This is what others see and this affects how people respond to us.

Getting to know yourself better means shedding light on what messages you are giving out about yourself.

1 YOUR VOICE

Listen in to the way that you communicate to others. This can give you valuable clues about your own self-image. What does your voice say about you? Is it clear, strong, calm, centred? What words do you choose? Do you communicate differently with different people? Why?

BABY TALK
Do you sometimes adopt childhood speech or expressions? When do you do this?

DITHERY
Is your speech scattered, hesitant, apologetic, unclear? What is making you unfocused? When do you do this?

BOSSY
Is your speech barking, brash, loud, overbearing? Why do you feel you are not being heard?

WHINING
Is your voice flat, defeated, filled with woes? How do others respond to you? Do you **expect** to be disappointed?

TEARFUL
Is there a quaver, a catch in your throat? What is making you sad?

ANGRY
Are there telltale signs of bitterness or resentment in your voice? What do you need to clear?

53

MUFFLED

Do you mumble or speak so softly that people ask you to repeat what you have just said? How much value do you place on what you have to say?

SPEEDY

Is your speech in short, sharp, clipped–off statements? Or do you rush on breathlessly? What would happen if you slowed down?

INTERRUPTING

Do you interrupt others often, or finish their sentences for them? Could you benefit from learning more patience? What are you missing?

2 BODY LANGUAGE

STOOPED POSTURE

Often, people with self esteem problems will be hunched over as if they literally carry the weight of the world on their shoulders.?
What happens if you straighten up? What do you feel?

CLOSED SHOP

A closed posture says `keep out' to others. Ask yourself, what is `dangerous' about opening up to life and others.

FIDGETING

How do you feel?
• Impatient?
• Anxious?
• Bored?
Have you found out how to just `BE'?

3 FACE FACTS

What message does your facial expression convey? Is it open, calm, friendly? Is it closed down around pain, hurt, anger? How will your face become `set' when you're older? What would happen to your face if you felt better? What if you smiled more?

4 ACHES AND PAINS

New research in the area of health is recognising what early cultures have understood for centuries - that the body/mind connection is very powerful indeed.

When we look at the possibility of illnesses having an emotional basis, or, at least, a physical vulnerability being aggravated by emotional stress, this opens up a whole new way of understanding what ails us and what our blocks are, and returns us to the power to initiate our own healing.

Here is an overview of the areas of the body and the emotions that may be linked to them. Use this as 'food for thought' about your possible blocks.

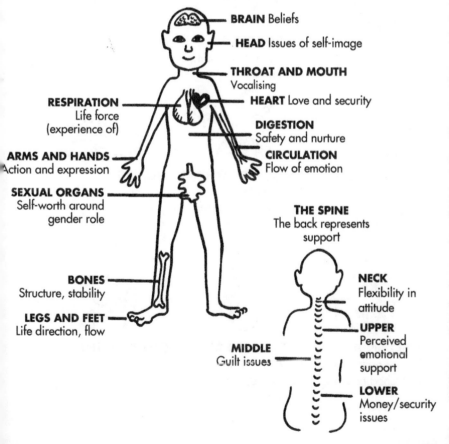

BRAIN Beliefs

HEAD Issues of self-image

THROAT AND MOUTH Vocalising

RESPIRATION Life force (experience of)

HEART Love and security

DIGESTION Safety and nurture

ARMS AND HANDS Action and expression

CIRCULATION Flow of emotion

SEXUAL ORGANS Self-worth around gender role

THE SPINE The back represents support

BONES Structure, stability

NECK Flexibility in attitude

LEGS AND FEET Life direction, flow

UPPER Perceived emotional support

MIDDLE Guilt issues

LOWER Money/security issues

55

Let's look at some common ailments and see what they tell us.

ANXIETY
Not trusting the flow of life. Resisting change. Accepting powerlessness.

BURNS
Anger. You need to get to the deeper issue.

COLDS, FLU
Overload. Too much going on - a need to shut down.

COUGHS
Listen to me!

HEADACHES
Self-criticism, holding old limitations.

HEART ATTACK
Lack of joy and love. Giving but not receiving.

INDIGESTION
What can't you stomach?
What's producing fear?

LUNGS (BREATHING PROBLEMS)
Not able to take in life fully. Holding in, emotionally.

BUMPS
A problem requires your attention.
A reminder of blocks.

INSOMNIA
Fear or guilt over unfinished business.

EYES AND EARS
Obvious - what are you avoiding seeing or hearing?

OVERWEIGHT
Using food as nurture.
Feeling need for protective padding.

QUESTIONS

- What would you say are your major blocks?
- If a friend were to describe you, what would he/she list as your strengths and weaknesses?
- Where in your body do you hold your fear and pain?
- Which three words would best describe your
  - facial expression
  - physical presentation
  - style of social expression?

EXERCISE

Make a list of the illnesses and ailments you have had. Now study the mannequin on page 55 to assess what areas they relate to emotionally.

Can you see a pattern here?

MY STORY

I was having a bit of a dispute with my partner. We had not resolved it by the time he had to leave for work, and I still felt some anger.

Soon after, I began to do some ironing, when suddenly I burnt my finger, causing a painful blister.

Later in the day, my partner called me. We spoke for some time about the `issue', until it was finally cleared and peace was restored.

As I hung up, I bumped my finger. Magically, the pain, which had persisted all day, had *gone*!

THE OUCH FACTOR

Using criticism as a tool

CRITICISM

Criticism can leave us feeling exposed and hurt. But criticism, used creatively, can act as an extremely useful device for personal growth and change.
Let's take a look.

Say someone criticises you over something you just *know* you have no problem with ...

... at most, you'll be surprised, because you know you're good at that ...

... but you won't feel hurt. You'll probably shrug it off, thinking your accuser has lost the plot.

Now, let's try a different scenario.

This time, you receive a criticism ...

... and you feel an `ouch'! That **hurt**!

You might react in one of several ways ... angry denial ...

... a return of the same ...

... becoming upset - hoping for a sympathetic retraction ....

... or trying to appear otherwise.

But nonetheless, it hit the spot.

What's the difference between criticism A and criticism B?

Criticism A didn't bother you. You know perfectly well how to cook. It held no meaning for you.

Criticism B, on the other hand, hurt you, because you accepted that it was **true**!!

What was levelled at you hit the spot because it contained a belief you held to be **true** about yourself - otherwise it would have had no effect!

So, what can be done about this?

Well, you need to change your **PERSONAL TRUTH**!
Let's try that again ...

You could change your idea about what is a `negative' trait and turn it into a positive one.

For instance, being `sensitive' may give you creativity, insight or compassion!

You could work on your 'faults' and find ways to become less 'sensitive'. Perhaps you could think about how you respond to situations and learn not to over-react. Then being 'too sensitive' would no longer apply to you!

CRITICISM can give you vital insights into yourself and others. Remember the **BURIED SELF**?

A fair bit of criticism that is levelled at you may actually have a basis in truth. Try not to react, but take it on board as something to be conscious of, and work at.

Watch for the same criticisms that come up again and again. These may indicate your own unmet childhood needs. In this case, the woman feels overlooked, as she did in childhood.

Criticism that you level at another may actually indicate something you dislike in yourself (that is, something that was disapproved of in childhood). In this case, you may normally be a real fusspot, but very disorganised when it comes to paying bills, paperwork, etc.

You're so bossy!

This kind of criticism may involve a degree of wish fulfilment. What you criticise most in another may be the very thing you would like to have developed in yourself. In this case, the man may wish he could be more assertive and less compliant.

As we saw in *Living IT up*, however, whatever you criticise most tends to be reinforced in your daily experience.

I hate untidiness!

Suddenly what you dislike ...

WHAT YOU CAN'T HANDLE INSIDE YOU GET OUTSIDE!

... appears to confront you everywhere!

 Because you're **focused** on it!

Hello!

Now, I'd like to introduce you to an interesting part of your brain.

We'll make this a short introduction, because we get to meet him in depth later.

We'll call him **PRIMAL BRAIN** (or **PB** for short).

Essentially, **PB**'s main concern is survival. He is not terribly sophisticated. His department is the feeling, reacting and responding department. As a result, he's not too fussy about *what* he reacts to - if the impact is great enough, he'll take it on board. He has no sense of humour, of time, or what is real, fictional or imagined. He just **feels**.

Eek! Yeow! Mmm... Bleagh!

And, so it is with **CRITICISM**.

Feed **PB** criticism, and he'll take it **personally**!

That means *any* criticism ...

of yourself ...

... others ...

... the weather ...

... your car ...

... politicians ...

... **anything**!

Old **PB** takes it on board!

What happens?

You immediately tense up.

Your muscles tighten and *you* begin to feel far worse than whoever (or whatever) you're criticising! Feed yourself enough of this poison (such as the **IT** speak!) and you'll be **guaranteed** of a bad day (and you'll probably complain about that!)

The Antidote?

Remember that **PB**'s not fussy. Whatever has the greatest impact, hits the spot (past or present)! Praise flicks a switch in **PB** and you immediately begin to relax. It doesn't matter *where* the praise is directed – inwardly to yourself or outwardly to others or things or events – it will have a calming effect.

You don't even have to speak! Just think it. **PB** will hear.

Learn to increase your appreciation of what you like and tolerance of what you don't like.

CRITICISM KILLS
PRAISE HEALS

What if YOU'RE being criticised?

Immediately negate the impact of the criticism by praising yourself. If you don't **fear** criticism it breaks the spell. Make it automatic, like saying 'Bless you' when someone sneezes. **PB** will stay calm and so will you.

'POSITIVE' CRITICISM

Pretty well all criticism levelled at others is self-serving. It deflects attention away from what we cannot tolerate in

ourselves, or what we do not want revealed to others. To put another down (however 'nicely') gives us a momentary sense of superiority to cover our own inadequacies.

However, if we did not feel threatened, we would not have to win power this way. Sometimes, we genuinely believe our criticism is helpful!

However, there *are* times when we are asked to give an opinion and we'd like to tell the truth. Well, keeping old **PB** and the greatest impact thing in mind, here are some ways to offer feedback.

Usually, as a rule of thumb, **PB** will retain what he's left with *last*.

EXAMPLE 1   THE TURNAROUND
Here is the usual pattern:

PB Just received a wet fish in the face!
Now let's try turning it around.

The advice, given in this way, seems less like criticism. The listener is left with an upper and not a downer.

EXAMPLE 2   THE CUSHION

The effect is softened by surrounding the criticism with praise.

In both cases, the listener is more likely to be open to your view if it is handled with care.

Unfocused Criticism

This type of criticism involves a sweeping statement and an unfocused generality.

Unfortunately, if your self-esteem is low you will tend to assume a guilty position without realising you do not have the full picture of what it is you are feeling guilty about!

Here's an example:

What's your immediate conclusion?

You've jumped straight to the negative assumption!

There are four steps to take in dealing with unfocused criticism:

1 ASK FOR SPECIFICS

What *does* the person **mean**?

The meaning needs to be defined and clarified.

Don't **assume** that you know the meaning. This asks the person making the statement to be clear in their own mind. too.

2 GET OUT OF GUILT

Is this the whole truth or the other person's interpretation?

You have been given a broad statement. Think about it. If you have become more selfish, did you *need* to?

Perhaps *sometimes* you are selfish, but mostly you're a good person. *You* judge (then return to Step 1).

3 OWNERSHIP

In what way is that a problem for you?

Again, this places the onus on the accuser to think about where *they're* coming from. *Whose* problem is it? Ask for clarity.

4 SOLUTION

How do you think we can resolve this?

Invite the person levelling the criticism to come up with a solution. You can **choose** to go along with it or not.

All of this is about being CLEAR

What do you mean?

Well, can you give an example?

If you don't know, ask!! Do you have the full picture or just a vague idea? Are you fully **clear** on what is being levelled at you?

And if the answer is still vague, ask again!

What changes would you like to see?

BEING CLEAR MEANS
NO GUESSWORK!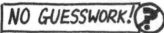

Get clear on what is expected. Get answers. **Find out!**

- It is *your* responsibility to get *all* of the information you need.
- It is *your* responsibility to state your limits.
- It is *your* responsibility to make yourself heard and understood.
- If *you* have a problem, it is *yours* to fix.
- If it is not *your* problem, don't own it!

67

QUESTIONS

- What do I criticise most in others?
- When do I do the thing I'm criticising in another? Is there a connection here?
- What criticisms are most often levelled at me?
- Is what I am most criticised for necessarily a bad thing?
- What should I do about what I am being criticised for?
- Is it in my *own* interests to change?

EXERCISE

Try role-playing with a friend before you have a difficult encounter with someone who is normally critical of you.

Try to identify the times when you react without thinking it through.

Aim to reach a solution satisfactory to *both* parties.

MY STORY

The most common criticism levelled at me over the years has been the one I have used as an example in this book - too sensitive.

When I finally began to see this sensitivity as an important component of my creativity and empathy with others, it ceased to be a problem and became a gift.

Nowadays, in the (now unlikely) event of receiving this criticism, my response, would be: 'Hey, it's in the job description!'

NEAREST AND DEAREST?

Working with intimate relationships

Now that you have begun recognising your blocks, it is time to take a fresh look at how they operate in an area where you are most likely to meet them head on ...

... with your

Nearest & Dearest!

Your Nearest and (possibly) Dearest may include your parents, your children, siblings, other family members, friends, and of course, your intimate partner.

For the purpose of this exercise, however, we will focus on your `significant other' because, above all, this is where you come face to face with any unresolved pain, fear, anger, longings and, most importantly, your sense of self-worth.

- Who else pushes your buttons so effectively?
- Isn't this an arena for your greatest learning?
- Isn't this where your deepest resentments and resistances are played out?

Let's look –

In choosing our partners and friends, how often do we seek out the same kind of framework for affection that we experienced as children?

  For instance, if your father was cold and distant, chances are you will choose partners who are similarly aloof and undemonstrative.

And, sure enough, you will feel just as **rejected** as you did in your childhood.

Why do we insist on returning to this pain?

Is this just our low opinion of ourselves?

Well, in order to understand this, let's do a bit of **brain surgery**!

The mind tends to operate on two different levels.

Introducing
Reasoning Brain ...

... and here, once again,
is **Primal Brain.**

The **Reasoning Brain** is the part we use most in daily life. It makes decisions, forms conclusions, deduces, calculates and rationalises.

The **Primal Brain's** main task is survival and self-preservation.

Here are the main attributes of these two levels of thinking.

REASONING BRAIN

- time-based
- aware of the five senses
- focused on one thing at a time
- prioritises where to focus attention
- makes choices about the way events are perceived.

PRIMAL BRAIN

- timeless (what was, still is)
- makes no distinctions between what is real or imagined (whatever **feels** true **will** be true)
- has no sense of humour
- works on anticipation or recollection of **sensations**
- seeks self-preservation and pleasure.

Lets look at them in action:

Here you are, happily using your **Reasoning Brain** to do your day's work. He hasn't arrived! You try

Then, your **Reasoning Brain** remembers that 'HE' is coming to pick you up. **PB** begins to give you warm, fuzzy feelings in response to the memory of HIM!

calling. He's not there!

Primal Brain is recreating

Reasoning Brain does its very best to kick in here - you **know** there are a million good reasons why he's late.

But it's no use. Old **Primal Brain** has zoomed straight back to childhood. You are five years old and you feel abandoned.

the environment of childhood, and hence, the same yearnings, and, as a result, the same pain.

Your suspicions were correct, your boyfriend is a notorious cheat and once again he's betrayed you?

Wait! Isn't **Primal Brain's** primary function **self-preservation?** Doesn't it seek out **pleasure?** Then what are you doing with ...

Well, old **PB** is not as masochistic as it may first seem ...

... It is actually **recreating** the hurts of childhood to **heal** the wounds and **resolve** unfinished business. It is seeking the pleasure of completion and wholeness. It is trying to reclaim the

BURIED SELF

Let's see how this operates with **Romantic Love** ...

Along with the yearnings of **PB**, you begin your search ...

... you carry with you a mental checklist of qualities you find desirable ...

... many of these qualities will be a blend of your parents' qualities, and, interestingly, you will usually choose someone as attractive/intelligent/caring/honest, etc. as you **deem** yourself to be!

OK. So your eyes have met across a crowded room and all that stuff. It's love!

Actually, it's more like **lust** at this stage! Old **PB** is back with the dinosaurs and the search for a mate suitable for the continuance of the species *and* we're back to seeking out childhood nurture.

Anyway, it feels good! All the endorphins begin to fly around your system. The world looks great. You're smiling and happy.

Best of all, you feel better about *yourself*. Maybe you *are* adorable after all!

You're both now on your best behaviour. You are the perfect mate - caring, thoughtful, loving and kind ...

And, at first, you go to great pains not to be seem **needy**, but nurturing.

No wonder he loves you! You're so attentive, so giving and unselfish!

Well ... maybe. But in fact, in the end, you are there for your *own* needs, not your lover's, as you will see. This is about **PB**'s quest to heal *your* wounds, not his/hers.

Because, sure as eggs ...

... things change ...

... we start to care less about giving ...

... and more about **getting**

Trouble in Paradise!

Expectations become higher ...

... you find a multitude of faults you want to change in your partner ...

... and what was once endearing is no longer.

You're not wearing that are you?

But you used to love my music!

Suddenly, the man of your dreams has become Freddy Krueger!

SO WHAT HAPPENED?

Well, remember how you came to choose your partner?

In recreating your childhood, you have chosen a partner who reflects your parents' positive *and* negative traits - traits that you have also inherited!

SO

Your partner serves as a mirror. What you like or don't like in your partner tend to be the things you like/don't like in yourself!

Sometimes, too, there can be a degree of wish fulfilment in your choice of partner, filling in the gaps you believe exist in your own personality.

If he's a **Party Animal** and you're retiring ... maybe you would actually like to be more outgoing!

75

However, # The Honeymoon's Over

At this stage, you've exhausted all the avenues. You've tried reasoning, bargaining, withholding and threatening, but there seems to be little hope.

But hold it for a second! Before you walk out, think about why you're in this relationship ...

TO HEAL YOURSELF!

Are the old patterns still in place?

Are they likely to repeat again even with a different partner?

Have you worked to resolve them in *this* relationship?

Perhaps a little more conscious work would help.

Let's take a look:

GET OUT OF THE ILLUSION

This is *not* a fairytale. The hero is not here to fill your needs - that is *your* job!

No one can rescue another.

Secondly, what you see is what you get! The person you met is going to remain the person you met, however much you want him/her to change!

And the object of your desire who was meant to answer all of your prayers ...

... has just as much of the wounded child inside as you do!

76

ACCEPT THE DIFFERENCES

Be very clear about the person you see.

In what ways do they reflect *your* strengths and weaknesses, biases and qualities?

Accept differences between your characters as *essential*.

Your partner is not here to please or impress you, but to *grow* with you.

CO-OPERATE

Be clear that your purpose in being here is to heal

yourself. Same for your partner. When you hit a sticking point, **help** each other work it through. **Assist** each other in healing and growth.

OWN YOUR OWN STUFF

When something your partner does annoys or frustrates you, take a moment to look to yourself first.

- Why do you have difficulty in accepting this?
- What does this remind you of from the past?
- What **feelings** have surfaced?
- When do you do the same thing?
- Is this annoying because he/she is not living to *your* rules but his/hers?
- What is the **real** issue here?
- How would your partner be seeing it?

AND WHEN NONE OF THIS WORKS ... **Let it go.**

Accept the reality that this person cannot or will not love you in the way you want. Release him/her to be who he/she *actually is*. Stop allowing what you *can't* have to control your life. Let go.

QUESTIONS

- If you look back over your choice of partners, what pattern has been repeated?
- How do your partnerships reflect your relationship with your parents? In what ways are they significantly different?
- If your partners and friends are a reflection of you, what strengths and weaknesses do they reveal?
- What is your primary management style in relationships?

EXERCISE

Close your eyes and relax deeply. Bring up a picture of your loved one into your mind.

Try to **become** your loved one. Feel him/her breathing and imagine you are seeing through his/her eyes as he/she looks at you.

Try to see what your partner sees - what causes frustration, but also what is **loved** in you. Try to **understand** that both parts are **essential**. Both the unpleasant and the beautiful exist because you are you. And you are loved **for who you are**.

MY STORY

My relationship with my father was played out over and over through my life. Cool, distant and `difficult' men were attractive - nice guys were boring. My only understanding of affection was that you had to **struggle** for it.

That, of course, never worked. It took *years* to figure out that I deserved better, which was *my* lesson.

THAT WAS NO ACCIDENT!

The use of coincidence

- How often have you been thinking of someone you haven't seen for a long time, and out of the blue, they call you?

- How often have you worried that your money will not stretch when suddenly an unexpected cheque appears?

- How many major events in your life have been steered by a surprise turn of events?

Were these things just **COINCIDENTAL?**

When we see no order or pattern to our lives, we tend to perceive events as random - sometimes good luck comes our way, sometimes bad.

But if we take a broader view, we begin to see an interesting pattern within these apparent twists of fate, simply by being **CONSCIOUS** of them!

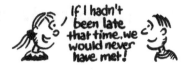

We tend to recall only major coincidences, but actually smaller `synchronicities' occur on a far more regular basis than we notice at first.

Interestingly — **THE MORE YOU WATCH FOR COINCIDENCES THE MORE THEY HAPPEN!**

If all we have to do is **tune in** to coincidences to have them occur more often
then surely ...

THEY MUST HAPPEN ANYWAY!

If we return to our list of possibilities, we find one that says `**Everything happens for a reason**'.

If we can accept that our time on Earth is a schoolroom, then turns of events would function to position us in the right place at the right time for the greatest learning.

A higher level of freedom and control can arise from adopting the idea that we actually create our own circumstances.

HOW?

☆ Instead of feeling like helpless victims of **Fate**, we begin to look for the reasons for being in a particular situation and for what needs to be addressed in order to move on.

☆ We *go along* with events, rather than resisting and feeling stuck as a result.

☆ We begin to live life as an adventure, rather than an ordeal. We begin to examine events for clues and insights to use for growth and empowerment.

☆ We adopt a more expansive view of others, seeing them as instrumental to our own progress rather than sources of aggravation, frustration, pain or disempowerment.

☆ We accept more responsibility for what happens to us, rather than searching for someone or something to blame.

In fact, it could be said that, if all events have a purpose, then there *are* no **COINCIDENCES** or **ACCIDENTS** - only scene shifts, entrances and exits in the grand opera of life!

It could also be argued that coincidences or accidents are simply departures from the **expected outcomes** in any situation. Perhaps our subconscious is leading us in certain directions which coincide with the direction of others' subconscious and we intersect at certain points.

In any event, developing a consciousness of certain patterns in your life, relying on your intuition and becoming more aware of connections can serve as valuable tools for adding order to your life.

USING COINCIDENCE

Decision-making is one area in which taking note of linked or `fortuitous' connections can be very effective.

HOW TO DO THIS

1 CENTRE YOURSELF

Resist making decisions when you feel hurried, tired, angry or agitated. Wait for calm. There is *nothing* that can't wait if you think in terms of your whole life! (An exercise in letting go!)

2 TRUST YOUR INTUITION   **3 PICTURE WHAT YOU WANT**

Close your eyes and note what your inner voice tells you. Unlike the **IT** voice, your intuition will be in the form of a calm idea coming through. If the message is clear, heed it. If not, try again later. Learn to trust that you *have* wisdom and that you *will* get the answer.

We are often clearer on what we *don't* want than on what we *do* want! Visualise where you would like to be as a result of your decision. What is the outcome? Imagine it in full technicolour. Make it real.

4 START THE BALL ROLLING

Having worked out the direction you'd like to head in, begin to take **active steps** to set things in motion.

Write a letter, make a phone call, get a brochure, etc.

5 THEN, LET IT ROLL!

Now, sit back and simply watch what happens.

Notice how things unfold.

Is everything going smoothly? Are there hitches? Are other possibilities coming through?

What are you seeing, hearing, reading, noticing in regard to your decision?

What clues are you getting?

CLUES

- Reading material
- Conversations
- Unusual mail, visits or phone calls
- `Chance' encounters
- Accidents
- Slogans, logos, graffiti
- Being delayed
- Arriving early
- Full bookings or sudden cancellations
- Trouble with machinery, car, phone, etc.
- Losing keys, wallet, etc.
- Encounters with strangers.

6 SURRENDER OUTCOMES

If it all goes like clockwork, **GREAT**! If not, if it's all terribly blocked ... **LET IT GO.** This is not always easy - especially if you had your heart set on something. But watch what arises as a result. Be **curious**, not cross!

Well, I tried all that and the outcome was a DISASTER!

Sorry to hear that. What happened?

I decided to move house. Everything went fine and I got the house I wanted.

Congratulations!

Yeah, right! I was burgled and mugged in the FIRST WEEK!!

Well sorry, I didn't guarantee happy endings, did I?

Well, no, but...

OK, I know it was tough. But what happened then?

Well, I did have insurance and...

And?

Well, after I was mugged, I started thinking about things.

Like?

Like, what's important, you know? I mean my LIFE had been in danger!

Yes. What did you decide?

I decided to finally move out of the city. I've always wanted to!

And how did that go?

Well, a friend happened to be selling his place and my insurance cheque came in, so I bought it!

And now?

Actually, I'm happier and more relaxed than I've ever been! I don't see possessions as being so important, either!

Thank you. I rest my case!

What is thrown at us can seem harsh or unfair at times, but essentially what you *need* may not be always what you *want*.

Our friend on the previous page *needed* to have his life endangered to fully recognise its worth. Most certainly, this would not have been what he *wanted*, but the impact was enough to completely change his attitude for the better.

Coincidences happen on many levels, but we tend only to recall those that seem to place us in a fortunate position, by our **existing standards**.

But misfortune in itself can, indeed, be fortunate, if the end result is a greater appreciation of who you are, and what you have.

Whether you stay **STUCK** in misfortune, or ride the waves of change and growth is up to you. But change is inevitable.

If only we had been brought up to value **CHANGE** more than we value **PERMANENCE**! How much more smoothly our lives would flow, if we were taught how to let go, move on, detach from outcomes and a belief in limited supply!

Instead of exhausting our energy shoring up against the uncertainties of tomorrow, we could be spending it on exploring the adventure of today!

And it **IS** an adventure!

Life can become **EXCITING**, a treasure hunt, when you begin to expect the unexpected!

Let's see what happens if you have a **PROBLEM**.

Say you've been having **huge hassles** with your boyfriend.

You've tried just about everything and right now you're completely confused about whether to stay and keep trying or to leave him, and get on with your life.

HERE'S WHAT TO DO.

1 ADMIT YOU'RE CONFUSED

I really **don't know** what's best!

When we keep pushing for a solution in a confusing situation, we can tend to become further buried in the problem. Give in! Admit you haven't got the answer ... **yet**.

2 GIVE IT AWAY

OK, whatever happens. I'll go with it!

Give away the outcome. Let things unfold as they will.

You might want to set a time limit on events - say by next week. Meanwhile get on with your life, **trusting** the answer will come.

3 WATCH WHAT HAPPENS

RING RING

Something will happen. The phone will ring, or there'll be a letter, or perhaps there will be silence, which will be a kind of answer in itself. You'll have your solution.

ABOUT ACCIDENTS

Accidents are usually wake-up calls.

You're bumbling along on some tangent that needs a shift in direction, or you need to be pulled up short to review the direction you're headed in.

Say you're at a dinner party. You're right in the middle of a story ...

... when suddenly, you spill wine all over your dress!

What were you about to say? Was it in your own best interests? If you could pick up the thread, would you? Does this warrant a rethink?

Accidents, especially those involving physical injury, are a means by which the psyche shocks you out of your trance, galvanising you into healthier action.

The more major the accident, the less you've been paying attention! There have probably been a lot of minor hints that you've been ignoring along the way, and its taken *this* to **wake you up.**

Accepting that you actually **create** what happens to you can feel rather confronting at first, but in time, you may recognise certain patterns of thinking that have accompanied events.

You may be equally surprised to find that, if you alter your thinking to a more positive outlook, you are less prone to illness or injury!

While some challenges appear in our life scripts to push us forward, we can sometimes pull other painful events toward us by our *own doing*.

It feels like an accusation to say that you 'took part' in a crime perpetrated against you, or an apparent injustice that has befallen you.

But, I am relying on you to remain **open** in your thinking.

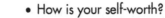

Let's put it this way-

This is *not* to say that you are to **blame** and the other party is **innocent.** But perhaps both of you were operating at the time on a **less conscious** level, which invited in this interplay.

Let's take a look-

Say you were the victim of violence.

- How is your self-worth?
- Do you live life believing that you are **fully worthy** of respect, love and happiness?
- Do you invest your trust in others wisely?
- Do you believe in life being hard?

If someone has stolen from you -

- Do you often feel 'ripped off' by life?
- Do you find yourself feeling resentful that you are constantly giving more than you get in return?
- Are you overly concerned about losing possessions? Or ...
- Are you uncomfortable about being prosperous?

Being controlled by another or by events in any way, means that you have **allowed** yourself to **be controlled**.

This is a game, and your part in it **allows it to continue or not.**

DISENGAGE from the game and it will **stop!**

If you give too much - **stop!**

If you allow yourself to be bullied, put down, coerced, cheated – **stop!**

But this will require all of your courage to be **truthful** with yourself about the part that **you** play in what happens to you. Not easy!

You may have heard of **KARMA.** This is about **cause** and **effect.** It is not some mysterious Eastern concept. It makes sense. In other (Western) words

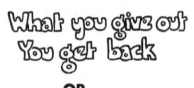

What you give out
You get back

OR

What goes around
comes around

Karma works in the following way. Whatever is unfinished, unresolved or incomplete will come around again until it is finished, resolved or completed.

It also means that whatever motives we use to acquire something, will be returned to us, in kind.

Say you cheat to get ahead.

Chances are you'll be cheated of your success or success will not bring joy.

It is a wonderful form of universal justice. If we take this on board, and someone *has* done wrong by us, we need do nothing to `get back'. At some stage they'll have to work it through. It is no longer your problem. No `revenge' is required.

MOTIVES AND RESPONSES

VIOLENT means - VIOLENT RESPONSES
RUTHLESS means - RUTHLESS RESPONSES
HELPFUL means - HELPFUL RESPONSES
SELFISH means - SELFISH RESPONSES
PEACEFUL means - PEACEFUL RESPONSES
And so on.

None of what you look at here is about **BLAME.** Questioning your role in events means that you are prepared to acknowledge your weaknesses in order to **LEARN** from them, **STRENGTHEN** them and **HEAL** them.

It means you are not a helpless puppet of **FATE,** but that you are a wonderful, complex human being who, with courage and honesty, is striving to grow!

QUESTIONS

- Under what circumstances did you meet your partner?
- Was your first 'impression' an accurate one?
- How did you find your job, your house?
- Can you identify a part that you might have played in a recent disappointment or hurt?
- How might you act differently in the future?
- What happened the last time a different outcome arose from what you expected?

EXERCISE

Start trusting your hunches. The next time you feel 'compelled' to do something, go with it, no matter how crazy it may seem.

Just see what happens, directly or indirectly, as a result of this hunch. A good rule is 'intuition first, backed by logic'.

MY STORY

I had been waiting for an important phone call, but it seemed that it wasn't going to happen, because it was days overdue.

I set off on an errand, only to realise I'd left something behind. I returned home and put down my glasses while I collected the item I needed. Ready to leave again, I looked for my glasses. I *could not* find them. I searched and searched, becoming annoyed, when suddenly the phone rang. It was the phone call! As soon as I hung up, I walked past a chair and happened to notice my glasses had fallen behind a cushion!

MIND OVER MATTER

Changing
mental attitudes

Back to our list of possibilities again, and we find: `What you **believe** will happen, will probably happen.'

Try this exercise:

1 Sit comfortably and slowly turn your head as far to the right as you possibly can.

2 As you do this, get a visual fix on something that is in line with the furthest point you can see.

3 Face the front again, close your eyes and, *without moving*, try to `feel' yourself turning your head *effortlessly past* the visual fix and all the way round till you are looking *behind* you!

4 Now, mentally turn your head till you face the front again, past the visual fix, *smoothly* and *easily*.

5 Now, open your eyes and repeat Step 1. How far past the visual fix did you get this time?

Wow! I can see the flowers

You'll be **AMAZED**!

So, what **happened**?

Quite simply, your reality was changed by **IMAGINING** that it was different!

By picturing yourself as being more flexible, you *became* more flexible!

This is the **POWER** of the mind. A power **you possess**!

Whatever you BELIEVE to be your reality will become your reality!

- If you **BELIEVE** life is tough, life *will* be tough!
- If you **BELIEVE** you'll always be broke, you'll *be* broke!
- If you **BELIEVE** you're limited, you'll *be* limited!

What do you **BELIEVE** about yourself? Do you **BELIEVE** you can have ...

- a totally equal relationship with someone who supports, respects, loves and nurtures you?
- a job that you enjoy going to each day?
- all the money you need without struggling?
- time to yourself, for yourself, completely free of demands?
- complete health and inner peace?

Can you see yourself having these things? What emotions come up around having what you dream of?

Is there even a kind of **PAIN** around having good things - being loved, being prosperous, being happy?

Is there a **FEAR** that if you allow in good things, they will only be ripped away?

Is struggle all you know, and therefore all you **BELIEVE** in?

Life *is* difficult, but how much *harder* are you doing it through your **BELIEFS** around a situation than the situation warrants?

Another item on our list of possibilities says:

`All suffering arises from our attitude to suffering.'

To demonstrate this, let's say you have something tough to go through. You can either –

Tell yourself over and over how hideous a situation is, thereby adding to your *own* difficulty in getting through it ...

OR

Take up the gauntlet and see the `hardship' as a task to be completed. Once you do this, the `suffering' goes out of it because you stop being a victim!

If you want a bad day, think this ...

GRANTED!
Today will be absolutely lousy! Enjoy!

Thoughts are powerful!

(HANDLE WITH CARE!)

Here's another example of `Mind over Matter` -

Say there's something you'd rather not do, like writing that report you've been putting off ...

VS

Something pleasurable, such as lunch with the new receptionist!

On the appointed day, you wake up with a dreadful cold!

Oh bno! By dnose is blocked up!

You feel lousy!

Oh bno! I dripped on it!

Oh it's nothing! I'm fine!

All morning, you struggle to keep going long enough to write the report ...

... but amazingly, by lunchtime, the symptoms are just a minor irritation!

We've all done it! But what's the difference here? You're still sick, but one situation has you feeling worse than the other.

It's when we **BELIEVE** something is onerous, painful, fearful, overwhelming or disabling, that it becomes so!

THE UGLY DUCKLING

Another powerful trick of the mind involves self-image.

When you look in the mirror, what do you see?

Do you immediately zoom in on the flaws?

If you perceive yourself as flawed, you are likely to project this. But if you think of yourself as beautiful, an interesting thing happens ... you actually **become more attractive**!

Let's see this in action.

If you believe you are flawed, you begin to close in on yourself.

You are more likely to stoop, frown, look tense and unhappy.

You try to compensate for or cover your faults with various devices of posture, make-up, clothing, etc., hoping no one will see your faults.

You become self-conscious and guarded.

But what happens if ...

Someone falls in love with you?

Someone thinks you're wonderful, beautiful, sexy, whatever, **just as you are**!

An interesting transformation occurs.

You actually become **MORE ATTRACTIVE**! Your gestures become more expansive, you have more energy, your expression softens and you smile more.

What if, instead of someone else doing this for you, you did it for **YOURSELF**?

Simply by recognising beauty in yourself, you allow the potential for that beauty to shine through.

Even smiling more, or being conscious of relaxing *your* face, can have a big impact, both on the outside *and* the inside. Research has shown that smiling actually calms us emotionally.

And this brings us to H✺M✺U☂!

Have you forgotten how to **play**? Has it all become so dire, so serious that you've forgotten to fit **fun** in there? Enlightenment can also mean to simply **lighten up**! Laughter and fun on a regular basis can be a far greater healer than any prescription!

Life can be joyous! **Seek out** the joy.

How much time do you spend rerunning the **pain** in your memory, keeping it alive?

What happened to all the good times? Weren't they just as real, just as valid?

Stop being so **EARNEST**. Goof around, play the fool, see the great cosmic joke of it all. Life's a game, an adventure. See the bummers as perfect **SLAPSTICK**, a big banana peel, or a cream pie in the face!

Automatically Ok

To significantly change how you feel, you will need to become an expert at self-observation. If you don't, you get caught up in knee-jerk, mechanical reactions.

BEEP!

Be especially watchful for old patterns of thinking creeping back in.

By now, you will have, hopefully, done a lot of monitoring of your self-talk through the work covered in *Living with IT* and *Living IT Up*. If so your vocabulary ...

will no longer include these ...

... and you will have replaced them with these.

• SHOULD	• EVER
• CAN'T	• ALWAYS
• MUST	• NO-ONE
• NEVER	• EVERYONE
• NOTHING	• EVERYTHING

• COULD	• RARELY
• COULD/CAN	• MOSTLY
• PREFER TO	• FEW PEOPLE
• SELDOM	• MOST PEOPLE
• FEW THINGS	• MOST THINGS

By now your **AUTOMATIC** choice will be **self-supporting**. If not, practise until it is.

Also remove -

And replace with -

• SELF-CRITICISM
• CRITICISM OF OTHERS
• ACCUSATIONS
• ULTIMATUMS
• UNREQUESTED ADVICE
• SERMONS
• 'NO I DON'T'
• 'I DO SO'
• 'YOU DID X'

• SELF APPROVAL
• ACCEPTANCE
• PERSONAL REFLECTION
• REQUESTS
• NON-INTERFERENCE
• HUMILITY
• 'I DON'T AGREE'
• 'I SEE IT DIFFERENTLY'
• 'I FEEL Y WHEN YOU DO X'

And remember - you can only hold **ONE THOUGHT** at a time!

MAKE IT A GOOD ONE!

QUESTIONS

- What things do you **believe** you can have in life?
- How many of your goals have you managed to fulfil?
- How likely do you think it is that they will be fulfilled in your lifetime?
- When you look in the mirror, what is the first thing you notice?
- How many times have you been playful or used humour in the last twenty-four hours?

EXERCISE

Keep a tab on how many times you use the words should, must and can't in one week.

Make a note of the situation you used the word to describe.
How could you reassess this?

MY STORY

Writing *Living with IT* was the best therapy I could have. In choosing to use humour as a means of illustrating such a painful experience for my readers, I was, in turn, re-evaluating the very nature of my **IT**. Because I could laugh (no matter how nervously) at my troubles, **IT** began to be `naughty' rather than sinister. I started to see **IT** as he was, my unruly child needing discipline and focus.

LETTING GO AND HANGING
IN THERE

Release
and
perseverance

It's easier to apply all of the principles that we've looked at when things are going smoothly. But when things get tough, most of what we know is best for us goes out of the window.

That's when you need to **LET GO** and **HANG IN THERE**.

LETTING GO

Let's look at this script of yours again. This scene opens at tragedy, or at least a major drama.

Whether this goes on page after page is not up to luck, but **how you choose to handle the situation.**

Often we get caught up in suffering because it makes us so damned **interesting!**

Have you noticed how people actually compete to have the greatest suffering? We do this because it offers perverse rewards.

You think you've got it bad? That's nothing!

Primal Brain (remember old **PB**?) is in action here. Remember how, as a child, if you were upset or hurt you were held, cuddled, stroked?

WAAH!!

- Suffering makes us noticeable.
- Suffering gets us attention.
- Suffering brings us the nurturing we crave.

The trouble is, if this is the *ONLY* way we believe we can be noticed or loved, it becomes a **profession**!

IT'S TIME TO MOVE ON!

Why? Because the attention that you may get out of suffering, instead of bolstering you, actually **DISEMPOWERS** you. You stay locked in a cycle of feeling helpless while being treated as helpless. You **give away** your power.

Oh there, there! PAT PAT

LET'S LOOK AT TWO KEY POINTS:

1 LIFE IS NOT EASY
Really get this.

LIFE IS NOT EASY

   GROWTH is in your script. That's it. No happy endings, no sailing off into the sunset. You may have tough challenges all your life, if you have to clear a lot of stuff, or you may have a holiday cruise.

BUT (BIG BUT!)

The more you grow, the less you see situations as intolerable. You **seek out** the good buried within the situation. You **stop resisting** and **resenting** and **get cracking**. Therefore, as a result ...

You experience LESS PAIN!!

Within every situation there is an equal potential for `good' or `bad'.
It's how you **see** it. It's the **memory** of pain that keeps it alive!

I lost him 20 years ago but it still feels like yesterday!

How **often** do you tell your sad story? How long will you keep it **alive**?

Your suffering can only last as long as the time you spend recalling it!

2 YOU CREATE YOUR OWN REALITY

Mr Sad, Mr Bleagh and Mr Joy are all neighbours.

Mr Sad, Mr Bleagh and Mr Joy's houses are all wiped out in a bushfire.

They have all lost everything, including a family member.

They have all shared an equal tragedy.

But what differs is **the way each handles it!**

It's my fault! I should have saved her!

It's their fault! They should have saved her!

Mr Sad lives out the rest of his life in guilt and remorse. He blames himself.

Mr Bleagh, meanwhile, blames others and the authorities. He remains in a bitter rage.

Mr Joy decides to work with others who have had a similar loss. Through this he finds a purpose for his own suffering.

What would YOU choose?
You can **choose** to hold on to a situation or move on, having gained valuable insights.

Oh I can't have THAT!

How much **JOY** do you feel you deserve?

How much are you prepared to do to feel better? **ANYTHING?**

Then, it's time to **SIMPLIFY** your life. It's time to **LET GO!**

Let go, Let go of... - a little more each day.

ANGER

Anger impacts on **you**. It keeps you locked into the past. It makes **you** the victim as much as the person you are angry with! Refuse to keep calling up the thought of what you're angry about.

What if I feel BAD?
FEAR

Fear is always **future-based**. It arises from **anticipation.** It consists of a **present** decision to feel a certain way in the **future!** For instance, if you fear rejection, you've decided to feel **rejected already**! You could choose another reaction!

I'm too wittle to do dat!
ENFEEBLEMENT

How often do you accept limitations? I'm too little, too lost, too confused, too stupid, too weak, too sick, too scared, too old, too this, too that? Who says? **You** do!

Let go, Let go of...

**RULES
GAMES
INSINCERITY
TRYING TO PLEASE
PUNISHING YOURSELF
BLAMING
CRITICISM
GUILT
DENIAL
EXPECTATIONS**

Let go till you feel yourself get lighter!

And, sometimes, when the going gets tough, all you can do is

HANG IN THERE!

As we've seen, growing through challenges requires accepting that they are an inevitable part of this growth.

The other part is *how* you work through them. If you do it kicking and screaming, you'll still go *through the challenge* only you'll do it **twice as hard!**

Sometimes things *do* feel almost unbearable. But somehow we *do* bear them, and we usually emerge the better for it, especially if we don't run, but **HANG IN THERE!**

And, to **HANG IN THERE**, you will need to become a kind of

WARRIOR

You have something tough to do, so it's best to get on with it and get it over with.

So, if you were a **WARRIOR**, what qualities would serve you best?

Oh dear, I'm not sure... maybe, but then...

1 DISCIPLINE

What is a warrior without discipline? A warrior has to undergo training to succeed, and **discipline** to apply this training under pressure. Discipline yourself to think better, watch what you say, and to get out of the knee-jerk reactions. Apply yourself.

2 DIGNITY

Hold your head up. Be a **proud** warrior! Don't fall for tactics that belittle you. Treat yourself and others with respect. Know you have strength, courage, wisdom. Give up complaining, nagging, blaming, regretting. It's beneath you!

3 DETACHMENT

Become a curious onlooker to events, rather than allowing them to overwhelm you.

Observe situations from the perspective of an onlooker. Be objective.

Take time to consider reactions and responses before applying them. Keep a cool head.

This way!

4 HONOURING YOUR OWN JUDGEMENT

You know what's best for *you*, no one else. You don't need anyone else's advice or opinions. You know what to do. If not, find out. Do not rely on *anyone* else's wisdom. That's theirs. Find *yours*.

CHARGE!!

5 ACTION

Theory is fine, but it doesn't get things done. A simple equation is: Time plus inaction = no results. Strap on your sword and **act** to change things for the better.

6 PERSEVERANCE

You may find that you have to hang in there for quite a while: OK. Just do it **ONE DAY AT A TIME.** Even one **hour** at a time if you have to. *It will take as long as it takes.* Forget about when it will end. You'll know when it has. Keep going till then. Never yield one victory! Never compromise what you've fought to gain!

7 INDEPENDENCE

Learn to rely on yourself to provide what you need. Do not rely on others to entertain, amuse, love, support, heal or nurture you. Others may not be able to provide these things when you need them, but you can.

Find them in yourself, first.

8 FREEDOM FROM DOUBT

A warrior relies on an unwavering conviction that he/she is strong enough, wise enough, and has enough of what it takes to succeed. Without this, the warrior will fall. Trust that all is exactly as it should be. Trust that you will be OK. I know it's been hard, very hard, but you must be strong indeed if you have been given big challenges!

It's like any game of skill - the better you get, the higher the degree of difficulty!

YOU'RE A WINNER!

QUESTIONS

- What is there in your life that you have trouble letting go of?
- What would happen if you did?
- How often in the past week have you talked about a problem?
- When faced with an ongoing difficulty, are you able to focus on the present, or do you visualise the problem going on and on into the future?

EXERCISE

Here is a very effective exercise to clear old anger and grief.

When you are alone and unlikely to be disturbed, stand in the centre of a room. Face one end and call into your mind all of the hurt, fear, anger, pain and sadness that you have known in your life. Really **feel** it, and let the emotions come. Cry if you need to.

When you feel you have cleared this, imagine that all of this pain is lying in a heap before you. Now wrap it up in a big parcel, tie it with string, and throw it away. That is the past. It is over.

Now turn and face the other end of the room. That is the future. Step forward and embrace it.

MY STORY

Whenever it all gets too much, I often call on the warrior idea, and, just by straightening up into that proud stance, I find the extra strength I need. When I find myself whingeing, whining or weeping, I suddenly remember the warrior, and I can't imagine her wasting one second on self-pity, like that.

THE PEACE PIPE

Applying love
and forgiveness

If you return once more to the possibilities on page 18, you will find the last one says `Love is an antidote to all suffering'.

How can love ease suffering?

What's **LOVE** got to do with it, when all seems unfair, uncaring or when others seem callous to our pain or, at times, even seem to add to it?

Here's what.

Why should I be loving when no one shows love to me??!

YOU'LL FEEL BETTER!

Let's get something straight. **REAL LOVE** is not for the **FAINT-HEARTED**. The benefits of a loving attitude can only come from **HONESTY, CLARITY** and **DISCIPLINE**.

AND REAL LOVE takes **COURAGE**.

Here's the other one!

It does not mean:

- lying down and playing dead
- turning a blind eye to reality
- being `nice'
- becoming a saint
- stepping out of the everyday world.

Why does everyone walk over me?

La La everything's sooo beautiful!!

Adopting a loving perspective in many ways means simply **LOSING RESISTANCE!**

For example:

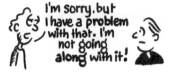

It means being **ASSERTIVE** *without* introducing **ANGER!**

It means **BEING CLEAR** in asking for what you *need* without playing **CONTROL** games to get it!

It means that you do not have to be **DEFENSIVE** because you've stopped perceiving **ATTACK!**

It means that, by applying patience, acceptance and empathy, instead of just **reacting**, you learn to **RELAX** about coping with `difficult' situations.

It means loving yourself and others enough to cease **controlling** by caretaking, fixing or rescuing others. It means attending to *yourself* first, so that you, too, do not impinge on others, and so that you *can* be strong and helpful if you are called on.

APPLYING LOVE INVOLVES:

- ♥ **caring** about everything you do
- ♥ leaving others alone
- ♥ **valuing** what you have
- ♥ taking **care** of yourself
- ♥ giving without conditions
- ♥ being **sincere**
- ♥ **accepting**
- ♥ **never assuming** someone has fewer feelings than you
- ♥ allowing others to be **exactly** who they are
- ♥ relinquishing judgement
- ♥ having **dignity**
- ♥ having **humility**
- ♥ investing **trust** wisely

Let's look at some of these:

♥ CARING AND VALUING

We take so much for granted. The fact that we have a life at all is pretty amazing when you think about it. And this incredible, complex, self-correcting body that carries us around warrants a moment's pause for thought. **Love** life. **Care** about it, and how you use this gift.

♥ LEAVING OTHERS ALONE

Honour another person's lessons as being their own. If you think they're making a mistake, **let them**. That's how *you* learned! Can you really say you've got it *all* figured out yourself?

♥ GIVING UNCONDITIONALLY

Give only when you expect nothing back. If you find yourself doing something for someone out of duty or obligation instead of a true desire to, you'll carry resentment with you. And that is *not* giving.

♥ BEING SINCERE

Not being true to yourself, and not being sincere to others rips you and them off. Sincerity means stepping out and revealing your true feelings, faults, strengths, doubts, etc. without games.

♥ FEELINGS

Being loving means identifying the fellow human being within. We're all just frightened little kids inside, trying to get by. You are, he is, she is. All we want is for *someone* to give a damn.

♥ ACCEPTING

This means that you accept where you are, how things are and others **AS THEY ARE**. Just go with it all. It's **MEANT TO BE** like this.

♥ HUMILITY

This means acknowledging you're not perfect and that's OK! It also means getting out of saying `I know'. Be open to the possibility that you don't ...**YET**.

♥ INVESTING TRUST

Basically, to keep walking back into pain doesn't mean you're being more loving ... it means you're being self-punishing! Loving another doesn't mean throwing away love for *yourself* !

And, of course, the most **LOVING** thing to do is to

OK. So you feel you have been wronged and, indeed, maybe someone *has* done something pretty lousy to you. What do you do?

Say your best friend has **stolen** from you ...

you trusted her and she broke your trust. At first you are shocked, then sad ...

... then you get **MAD**!

You decide you will *never ever* forgive her for what she did!

From now on, she **doesn't exist.** You will *never* speak to her again. She's **out**! She'll **never** get the chance to hurt you again!

Guess who you think about **ALL THE TIME**! The very person you want out of your life!

Month after month, year after year, the anger eats at **YOU**!

There's only one cure ...

115

FORGIVE HER!

What ??
NEVER!!

WAIT! I didn't say that you should make up with her, or even see her (walking back into pain is dumb, right?). Just **FORGIVE** her.

Why should I do that? It's her fault!

Maybe. But **YOU'RE** the one who's **suffering**!

Take a look at what **not forgiving** does to **YOU** ...

PAST

You become a **PRISONER** of the **PAST**. You constantly rerun the old movie about who did what. You cause **yourself** pain.

You are immobilised. Stuck in the **PAST**, you remain blind to the **PRESENT** and can't get on with the future.

What's wrong?

You are stuck in a **PATTERN**.
Because you have not forgiven (i.e. let go) you look for similar treachery in others. You no longer allow the trust that ensures closeness to others. If you stay in a rage, you screen out the chance to **REBUILD** that trust.

Unreleased anger has a lasting effect on *you* physically and emotionally, causing muscle tension, restless sleep, poor digestion, etc.

Can you see it is in your own interests to **FORGIVE**?

HOW TO FORGIVE

Most of what we have already covered comes into play here. Here's a refresher:

1 DIFFERENT SCRIPTS

It was in your script that your friend would betray you. *Why?* Did you invest your trust unwisely? Did your friend need help? What did you need to learn about friendship and possessions? What was in your friend's script?

2 MEMORY SELECTION

What you **CHOOSE to REMEMBER** will affect how you feel. No one walks around full of anger unless they keep calling up the **MEMORY** of anger.
You have the choice to feel better by letting the issue go. If **you** choose to hold the pain, then that should tell you something!

3 COMPASSION

A person who does a mean thing is not a person who feels good about him/herself. Compassion is about seeing past the act, to the sadness/ anger/ loneliness that prompted it. See others as two types - those who extend love and those who need it.

FORGIVENESS is an act of love for yourself and others that **FREES** you and others to move on. The sooner you get to forgiveness, the sooner you get to **PEACE**.

FORGIVING YOUR PARENTS

This is a special case. Your parents *should* have provided you with nurture, love and security. If they did not, the wounds will run very deep.

HOW CAN WE HEAL THIS?

1

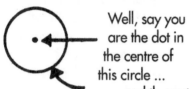

Well, say you are the dot in the centre of this circle ...

... and the rest of the circle represents your potential to be loving, whole and strong. In other words, your potential for spiritual development.

2

During your lifetime, by working at it, you may manage to fulfil your spiritual potential to this level.

3

Your parents (and others) for various reasons (economic, social, political, etc) may have only made it *this* far.

4

So, it figures you will need to be **EXPANDED** enough to embrace their limited realised potential, like this.

So this means asking yourself, how can I be **BIG** enough to accommodate this?

One way of doing this is to recognise what you have **LEARNED** from your parents. Did the **LIMITATIONS** of your childhood push you towards overcoming these limitations in your own adulthood?

Out of a determination *not* to repeat your parents' mistakes did you become ...

More loving?

More creative?

Less `driven'?

More determined?

But the one you need to forgive most is ...

YOURSELF

Forgive Yourself for ...

Not being perfect ... *no one* is!

Making mistakes ... that's how you **LEARN**!

The bad things you have done ...

I was STUPID to let that happen!

... or that have been done to you.

And, even for the **GOOD THINGS** ...

He'll leave me, I know it!

... you don't believe you *deserve*.

If you *did* act badly, **FORGIVE YOURSELF** by:

I'm sorry!

- identifying *why* you acted badly
- healing what lies behind the thing you did
- rectifying the situation
- not repeating it in the future.

FORGIVE YOURSELF for being just what you are: a complex, intricate, unique **HUMAN BEING** trying to grow.

QUESTIONS

- What do you feel guilty about? Have you forgiven yourself?
- Who do you still need to make peace with?
- What steps could you take to do this?
- Ask yourself, in a difficult situation: `What would be the *loving* thing to do?'
- How loving (to yourself and others) have you been today?

EXERCISE

LOVE: One of the most loving acts is to **LISTEN** to another. Most times we're only *half* listening.

How to listen
- Do not interrupt.
- Do not judge anything you hear as right, wrong, stupid, etc.
- Do not give *any* feedback unless asked (even uh huhs or yeses introduce *your* stuff).
- Let the person speak until they have said all they want to.
- Learn to be comfortable with silence.

FORGIVENESS: Write down the name of someone you need to forgive. Say three times: `X, I forgive you, from the bottom of my heart. I set you and myself free from my anger. Go in peace.' Repeat this exercise until you truly feel free of anger or resentment.

MY STORY

I was with a friend who was having a lot of trouble socially. She was often accused of rudeness and indeed, when stressed, she could be `difficult' - easily annoyed, irritable and short with others.

As she related her latest frustration with a colleague, she began to become agitated and angry. Purely on a hunch, I decided to try love. I cleared my mind of judgement and tried to see past her anger to the pain that caused it. Then, centring myself, I told her mentally that I loved her. Immediately she stopped mid-sentence, hesitated, then said, suddenly calmer, `I've forgotten what I was saying!' Amazing!

THE GETTING OF WISDOM

AHA!

Strategies for developing awareness

No matter how many books you read, theories you adopt, ideas you formulate or discussions you have, **WISDOM** can come to you only through **direct experience**, and through this experience becoming your **personal truth**.

 First, there is **information ...**

 ... and when this information becomes material that you apply to your own life, it becomes **knowledge** ...

... and when this knowledge is put into **practice** in your life, it becomes your own **WISDOM**.

AHA!

The next time you hear yourself saying ... *I know that!*

... ask yourself - Am I **living** it? If you still apply anger, fear, judgement, defence or control to be acknowledged, nurtured or supported, then probably you *don't* know **... YET.**

Only when you...

WALK YOUR TALK

are you living your wisdom

You may encounter the same notion over and over till *finally* it clicks into place.

Something brings this concept into the realm of your personal experience and brings it home.

'Don't judge others'... Well I don't. Not like Muriel, she...

Whoops! I was judging Muriel!

NOW I get it!

It has become your personal **truth**.

FOR EXAMPLE:

When you actually apply forgiveness to someone who has hurt you ...

... or you stop yourself just as you were about to join in on gossip about someone ...

... or you stop being **OBSESSIVE** about that deadline ...

... or you take the time to be fully **present** for another ...

... and you experience a kind of freedom from this, a letting go inside, a clean, clear feeling ...

YOU'VE GOT IT!

And as a result, the next time you experience the old thinking, you'll *feel* the contrast.

These 'flashbacks' - when you catch yourself up to your old tricks again - can be humbling and sometimes painful.

But they serve as reminders of *old* pain, that you are now working to clear.

So, how can you **access this wisdom**? Well, first of all, it means getting **BALANCE** back into your life.

A good way to do this is to allocate adequate time each day for the following:

WORK STUDY
REST and
PLAY SPIRITUAL PRACTICE

Let's look ...

Work is important, but are you working to live or living to work? If work consumes your whole life, what is it about your **life** that isn't working?

How much time do you give yourself to shut down, switch off and tune out each day? Isn't loving yourself about giving your body and mind time out to recharge?

Go ahead! Be **silly** at least once a day. Giggle, tickle, roar around, be a big kid. Do you **play** enough?

Or perhaps you play too hard. Again, **BALANCE**. Whether this is about exercise, entertainment, socialising or whatever, take a fresh look. How do you do this?

STUDY

You have the most interesting subject on earth **... YOURSELF**. If you want to change the way you think, compare it with what others think.

Try on new ideas, explore, open up to new knowledge. Read a book, discuss a theory, see a counsellor, begin a journal or just have a think.

SPIRITUAL PRACTICE

You may find spiritual nurture in watching a sunset or sitting in a garden. Or you may connect more strongly through prayer, meditation or a discipline like yoga. Fifteen minutes a day away from physical concerns, thinking peaceful or uplifting thoughts - that's all it takes to make a difference: to connect you with your higher self and a higher purpose.

Here are some practices that will keep you focused.

1 A BOOK OF WISDOM

Start a little book of lessons. At the end of each day, ask yourself: `What did I **learn** today?' Perhaps you read something inspirational or you had an insightful conversation or pivotal encounter. Try to pinpoint the theme of the day and your understanding of it. For example: `**RESPONSIBILITY -** others are not the cause or the cure of my problems.'

2 A JOURNAL

Keeping a journal is like having a confidante, best friend and counsellor at hand any time of the day. Use your journal to express and clear your feelings, thoughts, longings, dreams  and problems. Make it a safe place to work through your deepest issues. Only you need know what it contains, and when you look back at it later, you will be encouraged by this evidence of your own progress.

3 A QUESTIONNAIRE

If you feel blocked or stuck in a problem, or feel upset without really knowing why, work it through by creating a personal questionnaire. Allow your questions and their responses to flow out as automatically as you can. You'll know when you've reached the heart of the matter. You may find yourself crying a little when you hit the spot. This is fine. You will be releasing whatever is blocking you, and feel lighter as a result.

POSSIBLE QUESTIONS
- What do I feel?
- How am I blocked?
- What would make me feel better?
- What can I do to feel better?
- In what way am I holding this block in place?

4 SEEK A QUIETER MIND

Understanding a problem may be helpful, but understanding is only *part* of healing. Working too hard intellectually at being `wise' can often remove you from the very source of your own wisdom - your inner guidance. Only when you quieten down the din of thinking can your true **WISDOM** be heard. The seeking of a peaceful mind and a peaceful approach to life in itself solves most problems!

5 HEALING THE HURT CHILD

All the reasoning in the world will not stop the emotions of your hurt inner child rising in certain situations. A button gets pressed that jet-propels you back to your earliest feelings of fear, abandonment, denial, etc. Well into adulthood, that hurt child will still throw tantrums, sulk, whinge, cringe or wail. The only one who can heal him/her is you. Contact the child inside. Pour all the love he/she lacked onto him/her. Talk kindly and gently to the child. Heal the wounds. Then let the child go.

6 GIVE IT AWAY

If you haven't got enough of something - love, attention, even money - give away some of what you *do* have.

It's a bit like clearing a blocked drain to allow the natural flow of things to resume. The block you are clearing is your own `closing down' around your problem. In performing this act of giving, you **open up** to the possibility of receiving what you lack. In essence, you are saying `I'll **trust** that if I let go of this, more will come in to replace it.' See what happens!

And, finally, there are two age-old rituals guaranteed to connect you to the spiritual and your inner wisdom:

MEDITATION AND PRAYER

MEDITATION

We looked at meditation in some detail in *Living* **IT** *Up.*

In essence, meditation allows you to reach a still point in yourself that removes you from the clutter of thoughts, cares, and demands of daily life and allows your own peaceful wisdom to arise naturally.

PRAYER

Like meditation, prayer teaches stillness, trust and release.

However, while meditation focuses you on an inward level, prayer operates on an **active outward affirmation.**

In offering up a prayer, we set up, in our own minds, the possibility of a solution, a resolve or a change of thinking necessary to move along a current situation.

So prayer operates on a **psychological** level as well as a **spiritual** level.

PRAYER WORKS! But only if you have

FAITH that it will work!

FAITH means trusting that whatever is needed will come, that you **surrender control** of an outcome and **allow** things to unfold as they will, and go along with it all.

This can mean, of course that things may work out differently to what you might expect! There's a popular joke that demonstrates this:

BUT THE FLOOD WATERS RISE AND THE MAN DROWNS!

ARRIVING IN HEAVEN, HE PROTESTS TO GOD...

But I was sure You'd come and rescue me!

AND GOD REPLIES...

Blimey! I sent you a ROWBOAT, a CHOPPER & a MOTOR LAUNCH! What more did you want?!

What this means is that we need to be open to what *is* available to us, without getting fixed on something else.

In this sense, a desperate, angry or frustrated prayer is likely to go 'unanswered', because your desperation, anger or frustration will blind you to the sources of help that may be available to you.

HOW TO PRAY

Say you want more money. That's OK. Money can mean the difference between struggle and a sense of freedom. But think

about it. Is it the money or the **feeling** that goes with having enough money that you long for? Would it make you feel more secure, less stressed? Would it mean you could relax?

THAT'S what to pray for!

The FEELING   The THINKING
The HEALING   The LETTING GO ...

If you're upset ...   If you're worried ...   If you're lonely ...

Please help me to find PEACE.

Please let me THINK RIGHT about this.

Please help me feel LOVED.

... getting that new car may not bring you any joy at all!

Praying for **RESCUE** won't work either. Who is going to rescue you, except *yourself*? Most times, like our friend on the roof, the only danger we need to be rescued from is ourselves and our limited, negative thinking!

ANSWERS TO PRAYERS

Sit back and **TRUST** that what you need is on its way. All the strength, focus, patience, love and wisdom that you need is on its way ... **if** you **let it!**

OPPORTUNITY MAY KNOCK OVER AND OVER BUT IF THE DOOR IS LOCKED AND BOLTED HOW CAN IT GET IN ??

Phooee! It doesn't work!!

This means that if you stay locked in anger, fear, whatever, without **letting in** the possibility of feeling better, you'll stay exactly where you are ... **FEELING BAD!**

PRAYING FOR OTHERS

How can you stay **mad** at someone at the same time that you're sending them good thoughts through prayers?

This is a way of clearing and forgiving. It helps both *you* and others. Prayer can also be used to send help in your absence. Your prayer is a means of sending positive energy to someone in need of it, and, in this giving, you allow more to flow back to you.

Can you see now how prayer combines **all** that is on our list of **POSSIBILITIES**?

Be still, **TRUSTING** that your prayer is heard, by whoever or whatever you wish to direct it to ... God, a Divine Force or your Higher Self. Then, stay tuned.

QUESTIONS

- What is your spiritual practice for each day?
- How much time do you allocate in your life for peaceful, uplifting thoughts?
- How well do you know your own psychology?
- Would you benefit from getting more **peace** in your life?
- What active steps could you take to do this?

EXERCISE

Try asking for the **right words** in your dealings with others.

Just before answering the phone, talking to a friend or relative (especially `difficult' people), attending a meeting or visiting a client, take a moment to centre yourself around letting exactly the right words flow through you during this exchange with another. See what happens.

MY STORY

Like many people, I had for a long time a real problem with the idea of praying. It brought back less than comforting memories of the church and religion in my earlier years, which I had turned my back on. However, like many people, I still resorted to prayer when I found myself in a crisis. In time, I realised that it wasn't prayer that was the problem, but more the expectations I had of it and its connotations for me. Now I realise that all I asked for has been granted to the degree that I have **allowed** these things to be granted.

AMEN

OVER IT

YIPPEE!!

Summary

Whew! We've covered a lot of territory! Time to put it all together, eh?

Let's look at how all this might operate in three different versions of a situation.

Here's Betty ...

... and here's John.

Neither John nor Betty have done much of the work that appears in this book. They're just going along, not terribly unhappy, but not terribly happy either, like most people. They've never met, but they're about to ...

SMASH!!

... **HEAD ON!**

And, like most people, this is how they **react** ...

You weren't watching where you were going!!

WHAT??! You came straight at me!!

Oh yeah?! Well, you were in the wrong lane!

Oh come on! It's your fault! AND now you've made me miss an important appointment!

Well, You'LL be hearing from my lawyers!!

Not before you hear from MINE!

Now, let's say JOHN and BETTY are NOT strangers!

Are you all right?

Yes, I'm fine! Are you?

Yes, I'm OK. But this is a mess, eh?

Yeah. Look, what do you think happened?

Well, I went to change lanes and all I saw was you coming at me!

Hmm, changing lanes...THERE?! Well, I guess it's over to the insurance companies to sort out!

Hmm, well they're NOT QUITE blaming, but... Now here's a version where Betty and John have done some NEW THINKING...

Well, I'm glad we're both OK! Too bad about the cars!

Yeah. Pretty interesting that we both needed such a jolt, though!

Well, I had a tiff with my husband this morning. I guess I was still carrying some anger!

I guess you've let it out now!

Sure have!

And I was on my way to a meeting I really didn't want to go to!

Well, you got out of that!

Well, kind of... but it will probably be rescheduled. No avoiding it!

134

Well I'd better ring John. **This** may bring things to a **head**, but we need to sort things through!

Yeah, and we'll sort this out through the insurance companies. Obviously I need to do some **serious** thinking about my job, though!

 Wouldn't it be **great** if we **all** responded in this way? Why **don't** we?

BECAUSE

- We perceive others as **separate** from us. What's the saying? `A stranger is a friend you haven't met yet!' What if we were just as caring and compassionate towards those people we don't know as to those we do?

- We hang onto things. `But I worked hard for that car!' But it's a *car*. *You* are alive! You'll get another, or you'll take the bus and who knows what *that* will bring!

- We fear scarcity. `How will I ever pay for this?' I don't know. But you will. Think about it. Don't you always manage?

- We see events as outside our control. When Betty admitted to her anger and John to his problem with the meeting, they took responsibility and absolved each other of blame. Even if we can't come at the idea that we *caused* the accident, we could look at whether we were distracted or focused elsewhere.

Life gets simpler when you own what happens to you because *you* get to sort out what happens next!

Well, the world's been operating a certain way for a long time and, let's face it, there's room for some new thinking!

It may seem a bit lofty to imagine that by getting your own act together, you can make changes on a global scale!

But what if enough people made the changes you have~ if they became more aware, loving, peaceful, forgiving~ if they feared each other less...

... surely it would have to have some effect!
A better world... imagine!
Hey! ANYTHING'S POSSIBLE...

... and everything happens for a REASON and, who knows... maybe that's
IT!!